Fantasies of Love and Death in Life and Art

Fantasies

of Love and Death

in Life and Art

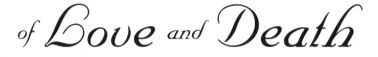

A Psychoanalytic Study of the
Normal and the Pathological

Helen K. Gediman

New York University Press
NEW YORK AND LONDON

NEW YORK UNIVERSITY PRESS
New York and London

© 1995 by New York University

Library of Congress Cataloging-in-Publication Data

Gediman, Helen K.
Fantasies of love and death in life and art : a psychoanalytic
study of the normal and the pathological / Helen K. Gediman.
p.   cm.
Includes bibliographical reference and index.
ISBN 0-8147-3068-x (alk. paper)
1. Love.   2. Death—Psychological aspects.   3. Psychoanalysis and the arts.   4. Psychoanalysis in literature.   I. Title.
BF175.5.L68G43   1995
152.4'1—dc20   95-7790
                              CIP

New York University Press books are printed on acid-free paper,
and their binding materials are chosen for strength and durability.

Manufactured in the United States of America

10 9 8 7 6 5 4 3 2 1

In loving memory of my mother and father,
Minnie M. and Louis B. Kornfeld

Contents

Illustrations

Acknowledgments

$\mathcal{J}$ thank my friends and colleagues from the New York University Postdoctoral Program in Psychotherapy and Psychoanalysis and the New York Freudian Society who have, over the years, exchanged ideas and made helpful comments on earlier drafts and oral presentations of the material on Liebestod fantasies. I owe very special thanks to Judith Isaac and to Martin Bergmann whose thoughtful formal discussions of the material at professional colloquia influenced its later development.

Portions of the section on Liebestod fantasies were originally published in the *Journal of the American Psychoanalytic Association,* which has courteously permitted me to reproduce them here. A particular debt of thanks goes to Harold Blum, who was editor of that journal at the time my articles were accepted for publication, and to some anonymous referees, all of whose confidence in my efforts at applied psychoanalysis and whose long and detailed comments were most influential in directing me toward the paths that later led to the present work.

Some of the ideas developed in this book received their first public airing at the 1990 Conference on "The Search, Passion, and Possession of Romantic Love," sponsored by the Washington School of Psychiatry. I owe a debt of thanks to R. Curtis Bristol and Stefan Pasternack, whose appreciation led them to invite me to participate in a most unusual and supportive interchange with them, and with Martin Bergmann and Ethel Person.

Over the course of three years, 1985–87, I had the rare opportunity to travel and study with the Forum for Psychoanalysis and the Arts, then headed by Bruce Sklarew, during which time I was fortunate to receive a solid on-site grounding in Italian Renaissance art from art historians Janet Smith of Florence, Italy, and Carol Ravenal of Washington, D.C. I thank all the members of that group for their discerning and helpful critiques during a presentation, in Orvieto, of some of my preliminary ideas on resurrection fantasies. A major mentor from that travel and study group was Ellen Handler Spitz, to whom I am especially grateful for her remarkable abilities to look at art through a distinctive psychoanalytic lens, and to enrich the interpretive discipline of psychoanalysis through the sensitive eyes of an accomplished aestheticist. I thank her for her patient critical reading of an early draft of the section on resurrection fantasies, and for her generous giving of her time and talents in conveying, by example, the difficult and disciplined methodology required of psychoanalytic scholars who attempt to cross the interdisciplinary boundaries of psychoanalysis and the arts.

I am particularly grateful to Joseph Reppen, whose careful reading of my manuscript and whose personal accessibility whenever I had editorial or publication questions were of unquestionable value in helping this enterprise to see the light of day; and to Janice Lieberman, whose enthusiastic sharing of her interest in psychoanalysis and the arts has been a constant source of pleasure and inspiration. Annette Weir, of Art Resource, New York, has guided me in my search through the art world for illustrations and permissions to publish them, and Paul Gediman has been of invaluable assistance in enabling me to master my computer and to produce a completed electronic document on my own. My editor, Niko Pfund, also of invaluable help in electronic manuscript preparation, has, through his faith and support of an interdisciplinary psychoanalytic endeavor, helped me to gain confidence in moving into territory where I can feel at home in attempting to communicate my psychoanalytic understandings in language that is comprehensible to a general audience.

I have turned throughout my labors to seek advice and exchange of ideas with Paul Gediman, a man of letters with an inborn psychoanalytic turn of mind. His writing talents, editorial skills, and good judgment have been unstintingly given, providing a steadying, comfortably restraining influence throughout all stages of the preparation of this book. My dedication of this book to the memory of my parents expresses my undying gratitude for their nurture and support of my development of the best that might be in me.

Introduction

$\mathcal{M}$otifs of love and death are found in the fantasies of certain normal and disturbed individuals, as well as in legend, art images, and musical themes. In these motifs, the sublime might well appear to be juxtaposed with the morbid, yet there is a broad range of love-death phenomena which, psychoanalytically speaking, spans a continuum between the normal and the pathological. This book addresses two kinds of highly organized fantasies of love and death: Liebestod fantasies and resurrection fantasies. Liebestod fantasies, expressing the passionate wish to die together with a loved one, and resurrection fantasies, expressing the wish to extend one's life and loves after death, are not limited to the tragic, the macabre, or to any given cultural context, though many of them, such as the love ballads of the medieval troubadours and the resurrection images in Italian and Northern Renaissance art, are typical of their times. An examination of literature and painting makes clear that the critical issues of love and death in art and life cut cross-culturally across time and geographical zones. Fantasies of love and death assume various manifest forms. Because their origins are to be found in normal stages of human development, however, they are omnipresent, if not universal, and have a variety of normal and creative as well as pathological outcomes. There are universal fantasies underlying the psychological normative and socio-theological traditions underlying the historical normative. It must be borne in mind, however, that even if a given product has as its roots the psychological and the historical normative, there can also be pathological variants. The level of ego functioning can best differentiate the pathological from the normal in these two forms of fantasies. The two classes of fantasy are distinguished by very specific, respective ego functions, which characterize them in both their more normal and their more pathological variations.

Part 1 of the book treats Liebestod fantasies, part 2 resurrection fantasies. My data sources for a psychoanalytic understanding of Liebestod fantasies are primarily literature, particularly the Celtic legend of Tristan and Iseult, among other fictional love stories, but also the libretti and music of the great romantic operas, including Wagner's *Tristan und Isolde*. My data sources for the study of resurrection fantasies are the images of Christ's resurrection and the resurrection of the dead in Renaissance and other painting and sculpture, and clinical material from the psychoanalysis of a man entering the twilight years of his life.

The term *Liebestod fantasies* was introduced into the psychoanalytic literature by Flügel (1953) to refer to fantasies of love and fantasies of death that condense into fantasies of dying together. The many versions of the Celtic legend of Tristan and Iseult are the basic Liebestod paradigm in the book. Rather than serving as the object of a psychoanalytic literary interpretation, the legend of Tristan and Iseult is a springboard for making psychoanalytic distinctions between normal and pathological aspects of love. This legend is about romantic love, a topic neglected in most of the psychoanalytic literature except for its connection with libidinal sexual development. It is also about death, and about the relation of love and death. An analysis of the legend allows for an elaboration of the normality of passionate love, which has, as a rule, been relegated in psychoanalytic thinking to the realm of the pathological as a form of sadomasochism, or to the pathologically tinged, narcissistic states of consciousness required for overidealizing the often not very love-worthy beloved.

Love has been conceptualized as romantic, sensual, sexual, affectionate, sweet, bitter-sweet, painful, and, yes, deadly. The deadly connotations were prominent in the Middle Ages when the ideal of romantic love was a love that was not consummated. Instead of the consummation of orgasm, lovers sought consummate feelings at the point of death. A central characteristic of romantic love in medieval times was the inability of the lovers to live without each other. The lover feared that life would not be worth living if the beloved were to leave. The union that lovers did not achieve in life is found in their anticipation or realization of their joint death. Bergmann (1987) believes that the English language has resisted the coining of an appropriate word to characterize this deadly aspect of love, so that the German *Liebestod,* or love-death, has acquired international meaning. Wagner's leitmotif has captured the essence of the love-death or Liebestod fantasy. Romantic love, however, has extended beyond the vocabulary of the Middle Ages. The romantic lover is no longer typically a knight in love with a married woman of higher social rank, the relatively inaccessible femme fatale. In the romantic love of today, it is no longer the unconsummated love that is idealized. There have been historical, social, and psychological transformations since the time when the sexual climax of orgasm was rejected in favor of the transcendental bliss of a joint death, which constitutes Bergmann's main argument that the Liebestod, or love-death, of romantic love was the substitute for orgasm in normal love. Yet, romantic love as human and normal survives. Many psychoanalysts identify its survival simply as a species of neurotic love but that is a narrow and limited view. Romantic love inhabits a spectrum ranging from the normal to the pathological.

Attractions of one individual to another have been characterized as platonic, as affectionate bonding, as with or without "chemistry," as healthy, sick, passionate, star-crossed, fateful, and yes, fatal. Some of the more deadly aspects of love and loving have been associated with the notion of annihilation. Lovers succumb, surrender, and annihilate their "selves" in the process of fusion with one another. This fusion can be benign, deadly, or anything in between. Not only has psychoanalysis shied away from the deadly, annihilatory aspects of passion, but its treatment of love, when it treated it at all, has been gingerly and reserved. Love has been seen mainly as sublimated libido. Yet, in the somewhat sanitized versions of psychoanalysis in the decades of the 1940s, 1950s, and even 1960s, annihilation anxiety referred to a dread of the strength of the instincts and rarely to the existential anxieties about the annihilation of life and the extinction of the self. One *could* find a complex latent foundation for the more intense varieties of love if one searched hard. Clearly, death is craved in the context of intense sexual passion in instances when it is considered preferable to the amniotic blur of losing one's sense of identity through merger with a passionately loved other. The strains of craved death from sexual passion emerge out of anxieties about the annihilation of one's sense of being a self existing separately from an enamored other. It is as though actual death and implied resurrection of the self were preferable to the love-death and implied annihilation of the self through merger and dying together.

Outside of psychoanalysis, particularly in literature, there has been plentiful speculation as to the nature of romantic, passionate love. In 1963, the more modern, and surely more romantic, novelist and literary critic John Updike, debated the views of the more ascetic Swiss theologian, historian, and essayist Denis de Rougemont. Updike tilted mercilessly at de Rougemont's stated notion that love and passion cannot coexist in civilized society without some dire and deadly consequences not only to the afflicted, smitten individuals but to the entire fabric of Western society. De Rougemont argued that romantic love is the celebration and pain of the involved individuals and not that of any larger social units. He was expressing a widely held fear that romantic love may come into conflict with ordered society. Indeed, romantic love traditionally has been regarded with suspicion by those not in its thrall, who find it foolish, narcissistic, destructive, deadly, and, unconsciously, enviable, because of the intense bonds that exclude the onlooker. To see others sometimes savoring, sometimes provocatively flaunting rapture, transport, bliss, and ecstasy when one is excluded provokes primal scene trauma, so that one dismisses romantic lovers as silly and mad. And it is not just the excluded spectators making social commentaries who fear romantic love. As Ethel Person (1989) sums it up, "rationalists" regard romantic love as a foolish if not dangerous illusion which creates impossible expectations in people and makes them unable to accept the limited good that *is* possible in relationships. They associate passionate love with "consumptive heroines, heroes wasting away with feverish desire, and deathbed farewells; with the overwrought, 'unhealthy' music of Wagner, Strauss and Puccini" (15–16).

In reviewing the normal and pathological variants of passionate love themes and fantasies, I have considered, in the field of art, the operas of Richard Wagner, such as *Tristan und Isolde* and the Ring Cycle, which contain musical elaborations of the Liebestod motif. My psychoanalytic thematic analyses have relied to some extent on the "pathographic method," a study of factors in the life of the artist, such as the psychological and social facts in the life of Richard Wagner that most likely motivated his inclusion of the themes of love and death in so many of his operas.

In studying Liebestod fantasies, much of the controversy between the critics interested in the normal and abnormal aspects of loving, falling-in-love, and being-in-love is included in updated form in this book. I expand an understanding of the normal as well as the pathological phenomena involved in that classical arch-romantic theme of one person's yearning to die together with a loved one. I explore the fantasy, held by many, consciously or unconsciously, that the proof of love is that one's lover shall wish to die upon one's death. Dying for the love or ostensible proof of the love of another is to be found as motive in double suicides, suicide-murder pacts, and the social pathology of such mass murder-suicides as the Jonestown massacre and the Branch Davidian tragedy in Waco, Texas. These dramatic variants extend my psychoanalytic research beyond the Wagnerian leitmotifs and shed light on the multiply determined fantasies underlying the yearning to die together.

There is more to romantic love than mere gratification of sexual desire and the presence of affectionate feelings towards another as a separate human being. De Rougemont believes that romantic love is more the handmaiden of death than of sexual and affectionate pleasures. This line of thinking might tempt one into the facile assumption that this is a terrible thing, for all the morbid sadomasochistic pathology that it implies. Romantic love, however, is more than a pathological aberration characterized by emotional excess and fatal outcomes. It is much more fruitful to view romantic love in terms of what it attempts to transcend. Person (1989) rightly grasps the issue of transcendence in asserting that romantic lovers grant more priority to the question, "Would you choose to die with me or to survive?" than to the typical defining question for those of less romantic bent, the conventional "Do you love me?" She concludes that, "whatever the deepest longing in love, it transcends a mere search for pleasure or the routine avoidance of pain, or happiness as conventionally described" (76). Nevertheless, conservative psychoanalysis traditionally has been leery of engaging the full-bodied passion of fusion, merger, and transcendence in love and death.

In this context, it helps to distinguish three related states: loving, being-in-love, and falling-in-love. This book will consider the continuum that ranges from the pathological to the normal aspects of passionate love, with respect to ego functions (see Bellak, Hurvich, and Gediman 1973) and with a particular focus on high-level creative transformations in "states" traditionally regarded as simply pathological. The Liebestod is characterized by the wish for "merger," symbiosis, and other forms of identification with the loved object. The outcomes of this wish may vary along the normal-pathological continuum, depending on the degree of ego control and regression. The essence of ego functioning in the Liebestod is merger with an object. Where a given Liebestod experience falls on the normal-pathological continuum depends on the level of ego functioning in that merger experience. The more normal merger states are characterized by oscillations, or flexible shifts in ego functioning, enabling temporary merging with the object, or loss of boundaries between self and object, while at the same time maintaining the integrity of the ego or self. In these variations, adaptive ego functioning is not disturbed, despite merger. States of passionate love are then not incompatible with object constancy and a loving concern for the object. Normative ego functioning and the capacity for individuation and object love insures against pathological loss of self-object boundaries in the amniotic oneness of being-in-love. Liebestod, then, in its normative sense, must be understood both as a fantasy and as a real, actual experience. The oscillations in adaptive ego functioning permit merger and reunion of two individuals whose separate identities are fundamentally intact despite temporary regressive merger experiences. Pathology occurs when a lover fails to resolve the conflicting desires for separateness and oneness. So, Liebestod in its pathological sense is characterized by pathological merger resulting from characterological or permanent ego function disturbance, particularly by uncontrolled regression to states in which self and object are experienced as fused.

Subjective feelings of merging and fusing with another may vary on a normal-pathological continuum according not only to level of ego functioning, but also to the degree of transformation of narcissism, from its more normal to more pathological forms. Merger states of the Liebestod have come to be regarded, especially by Bach (1985), drawing heavily on Kohut's ground-breaking discoveries, as altered ego states, specifically referred to as narcissistic states of consciousness. The merger sought in the passionate Liebestod states can be understood as "twin narcissism." As Kohut (1966) discovered, narcissism undergoes progressive transformations. There are, of course, positive and creative values in certain narcissistic modes of loving and the concomitant ego states they may activate in the overall context of ego-relatedness. We must look back to the earliest developmental stages of life in our search for the normal roots of the passion that sometimes leads to the despair and misery that have captured the attention of poets and artists. Traditionally, psychoanalysis has considered the state of falling-in-love or being-in-love to be a pathological state of heightened narcissism, derived from the earliest infantile experiences of fusion and merger with the mother. Passionate love and love-death fantasies have therefore been regarded as smothering the capacity for mature object love and the more tender, affectionate aspects of loving concern for others. They have also been seen as sadomasochistically based means of "raising the ante" of anticipatory excitement via passionately addictive and deadly states of intensely arousing stimulation. Several themes can be used to question these assumptions. The first is the idea of "twin narcissism," an idea which once assumed that loving the other as the self, or as a "selfobject" (Kohut 1971), negates a regard for the other as other. This idea expresses the one-sided view that this narcissistic mode of loving led to the psychological death of the human other in all of his or her uniqueness. In fact, narcissistic, and especially twin-narcissistic and object-related aspects of love, may coexist in the same person over a period of time. Freud's ideas on narcissism as well as those developed by Kohut in his early work on that subject both allow for that coexistence. Twin narcissism, and even the most extremely deviant states that passionate love manifests in both Liebestod and resurrection fantasies, have their roots in normal development.

In a study of love, it is possible to apply ideas in psychoanalysis to the topic of unbearable longings, of unsatisfied or unrequited passion. It was just such a feeling of insufficiency, wanting and longing that characterized the romantic love songs and novels of the French troubadours. As Bergmann (1987) paraphrased Schopenhauer, endless bliss is associated with the possession of one particular person, and unutterable pain is associated with the thought that the possession is unattainable. The normality or pathology underlying such yearnings is not a function of narcissism, but is a function of the extent to which conflict about merger with one's "twin" is resolved, and whether the temporary suspension of ego functions in the altered being-in-love state is feared or craved.

∾

The prevalence of particular death themes in Renaissance art representations of the Christ story inspired the selection of the second love-death theme, resurrection fantasies, to be developed in part 2 of this book. The theme of passion extends beyond passionate love, the Liebestod, to the Passion of the Christ story, particularly the sequential phases of the Passion as portrayed in Italian Renaissance painting and sculpture: Christ's flagellation and crucifixion; scenes of the deposition, entombment and lamentation; and representations of the opening of Christ's tomb and, finally, of Christ's resurrection. Themes of resurrection, not just of Christ but of all of the dead, the apocalyptic themes of the rise to glory or the descent to infamy of all the people who have ever died when the day of judgment comes, dovetail with the communally acknowledged and latent meanings of Christ's resurrection in the Passion story. The parallelisms in the meanings of the word, "passion," as used in the two contexts of romantic love and the Christ story are, to my mind, not accidental. The Passion of Christ contains within it a love story, albeit one that has not been treated as extensively in the psychoanalytic literature as the still relatively untouched topic of passionate romantic love. Sex, yes, sexual aberration, yes, pathology in the relationships of affectionate bonding, a limited psychoanalytic vision that Ethel Person speaks of as the "Ma and Pa Kettle" values of the mental health movement, stripped of the passions of the Passion and the Liebestod—these limited views of love as a simple vicissitude of libidinal-drive organization were the foci of psychoanalysis past. A present focus gains by including a thorough discussion of the developing themes of passion in romantic and other love-death connections.

It may seem odd to include resurrection themes under the heading of love, since they are customarily associated simply with death and coming back to life. But the connection will be more real than apparent as we discover that certain fantasies of resurrection contain ideas of being sensually happy after death, as in the condensation of Liebestod and resurrection motifs in "le petit mort" of orgasm. Despite the many points of contact between the two forms of fantasy, they will be shown to differ with respect to the ego functions that define their place on the normality-pathology continuum. In considering the differences between Liebestod and resurrection fantasies, the amniotic merger, or what Bach (1994) has termed "erotic haze," of Liebestod has to be distinguished from the essential narcissistic or egoistic character of resurrection fantasies. Liebestod fantasy, in pointing to a primal merger in which the self disappears, is qualitatively different from resurrection fantasy, which is future-oriented (not primal) and in which the ego is precisely what survives forever. Rather than the preoedipal symbiosis, fusion, and merger that are found in Liebestod fantasies, the hallmark of resurrection fantasies is the presence of phallic narcissism and self-assertion in the interest of restoration of the self and its perpetuation in immortality. Ego functioning relevant to resurrection fantasies is characterized by the assertion or preservation of the self with or without regard for the object. Normal self-assertion involves adaptive or creative transformations of narcissism, as in the wish for the survival of one's works, which does not involve an object, or in the concern for continuity and remembrance of one's self in the minds and hearts of future generations of "significant others." Pathological perpetuation of the self is typified by grandiosity in narcissistically driven preoccupation with defeating the reality of death. The narcissistic line of development, according to Kohut, parallels the object-libidinal line. There can be greater or lesser adaptive functioning in either line, characterizing the degree of normality-pathology. It would appear as though the Liebestod were characterized more by the object-libidinal line, and resurrection fantasy by the narcissistic line, but it shall be shown that this is not precisely the case.

An interpretive examination of the theme of resurrection from the vantage point of classical legend, theology, and iconography, particularly in its explicit images in the Italian and Northern Renaissance paintings and sculpture of the Christ story, can illuminate the unconscious meanings of a patient's resurrection fantasies. From the other direction, a psychoanalytic understanding of the resurrection fantasies of our patients should be able to expand the context for our understanding and interpretation of works of art in which the content is manifestly that of resurrection. An important thematic connection between ideas of love in life and love after death is suggested by the fantasy of sexual arousal in the resurrection of the flesh following its mortification. Death of the flesh is a theme expressing the narcissistic mortification that some men and women experience or anticipate, particularly as they get older. Resurrection fantasies, along with the symbiotically derived wish for the blissful merger of the Liebestod, serve as motivations in the quest for fatal attractions, particularly in the middle and later phases of the life cycle.

Although this book relies heavily on an analysis of love and death themes in literature and art, as well as clinically, in life, it is not an attempt at literary criticism. It relies, rather, on material from the disciplines of literature, history, music, art, and religion, in addition to clinical material, to provide illustrative data in support of the psychoanalytic hypotheses being advanced. In studying resurrection fantasies, the pathographic method is sometimes relevantly applied, for example, to aspects of the driven and melancholic life of Michelangelo that lent so spectacular a cast to his statues of Christ's death and resurrection. Universal or communally held psychological fantasies as well as iconographic traditions underscore the normative; idiosyncratic variations encompass the pathological. In addition to grasping the psychological meaning of critical aspects of the artist's life, therefore, the interpreter of art images must be informed as to whether a particular tradition of pictorial representation of a theme is characteristic or idiosyncratic before interpreting the image as a pathological expression of a universal fantasy.

There is a very specific positive function served by art, exemplified in the closing passages of Wagner's works, which relates not just to social reactions of terror and contempt but also to social reactions of a very adaptive order. In the Liebestod ending of *Tristan und Isolde* and in the combined Liebestod, resurrection, and redemption themes of the final acts of the Ring Cycle operas, *Die Walküre, Siegfried,* and *Götterdämmerung,* the central characters have died from the effects of demanding too much of life. The passionate emotional excesses expressed in the love duets, such as Brünnhilde's fearlessly throwing herself onto Siegfried's funeral pyre in the Ring's apocalyptic finale, represent, according to Tanner (1985), a critical way in which all great tragic art can help us to check similar impulses in ourselves. This positive, adaptive function permits gratification while at the same time checking unbound social expression: it is a valued compromise. The "overwrought music" of the arch-romantic composers, and the emotional excesses of artistic renditions of the Liebestod and the Resurrection, thus express adaptive as well as regressive ego functioning in the psychological states they are depicting. Even the romantic fantasies Wagner so brilliantly transformed into his great art have adaptive aspects along with their depiction of doom, gloom, and fatal attraction.

Fantasies of love and death are found to coalesce in art and life. They are expressed in the Liebestod and resurrection motifs chosen from works of art and contemporary clinical material, both of which lend themselves to psychoanalytic interpretation. The psychoanalytic meanings of these fantasies and motifs, as embedded in the arts as well as the human psyche, are arrayed with both normal and pathological aspects. In tying together the various phenomena depicted by artist, writer, musician, individual lover, or existentially anxious individual, an organic whole can begin to be discerned and shaped out of the love-death connection. Scholars and interpreters of this connection throughout the ages were never dealing simply with sensationally morbid themes, or with gross psychopathology, or with extreme social unrest. They were also—and always—dealing with events that could be ordered on a continuum of the normal and pathological. These events are related in complex ways that need to be articulated. Such is the major aim and purpose of this book.

Part One

Liebestod Fantasies

One

Reflections on Romanticism, Narcissism, and Creativity

*A*ccording to Martin Bergmann (1987), psychoanalysts always have been unable to explain the nature of love. But psychoanalysis seems to have borrowed from the Middle Ages, the idea that other than sexuality and orgasm, love is a narcissistic phenomenon. Not only is it based on a foolish idealization of the loved one, but as Plato said, on a feeling of insufficiency, wanting, and longing. In the Middle Ages, romanticism implied sexually unconsummated love. The songs of the troubadours substituted a consummation at the point of joint death for the bliss of orgasm. Endless bliss, a narcissistic state, was according to Schopenhauer associated with the unutterable pain at the thought that the possession of a particular person is unattainable. Such a painfully yearning love was often for "the double," a narcissistic love, which in most psychoanalytic developmental timetables may be older than heterosexual love. Goldin (1964) beautifully illustrates how a number of poets of medieval courtly love understood the similarity between narcissism and the worship of "the lady," noting that lovers only love themselves when they worship her. Looking into her eyes was as gazing into a mirror that pleased so much. Shakespeare mocked narcissistic love in *Twelfth Night* (1623), in which he dramatized how we love not what is but what we fools imagine exists. Freud (1914), less pejoratively, understood that we love others for what we believe once was, or we become dependent on the love object as idealized partner by living through him or her as though it were oneself we adored.

But does this narcissistic quality of love signify it as pathology or do we discover roots in the normal? The apparent conflict between narcissism and object love found throughout psychoanalysis and the love-death mythology of medieval courtly love was questioned by Freud, then by the work of Kohut. Kohut's (1966) theory that narcissism unfolds as a normal developmental sequence in its own right suggests new dimensions for the resolution of certain old controversies. One such controversy, of interest to poet and psychoanalyst alike, is embedded in the polarity of "loving" versus "being-in-love." Being-in-love is a transitory state, largely narcissistic, while loving is often experienced as a rational, more durable, "mature genital object relationship" (Bak 1973). Once the establishment of a narcissistic self is understood to be a maturational achievement paralleling that of object love, it is easy to see how states of loving and being-in-love both recapitulate earlier ego states and may coexist in the mature adult.

The contrasting views of two literary critics provide a springboard for the reflections put forth in this chapter. John Updike (1963) wrote a scathing and eloquent critical essay in the *New Yorker* on two books by Denis de Rougemont—*Love in the Western World* (1956) and *Love Declared: Essays on the Myths of Love* (1963). The controversy that sparked my interest was inherent in the discrepancy between Updike's and de Rougemont's views on narcissism as depicted in the myth of Tristan and Iseult. Updike's review was written nearly a decade before the upsurge of psychoanalytic interest in the many facets of narcissism. Today, his ideas are all the more salient in the light of our present understanding of a spectrum of normal and pathological phenomena encompassed by narcissism.

The essence of Kohut's (1966, 1971) position is that there is a separate narcissistic developmental line which is never outgrown but is, rather, transformed. According to this view, the narcissistic line of development parallels the object-libidinal line of development. Kohut's position, therefore, requires that we abandon the old view that narcissism is merely a precursor of object relations and object love and, thereby, a developmental stage to be outgrown. Instead, we must regard narcissistic libido as normally undergoing progressive transformations which are developmental accomplishments. This newer view can account for the simple observation that certain people who fall romantically in love—an expansion of the idealized or narcissistic self—are also capable of object love—of loving someone for whom he or she is, not simply as one wished oneself to be, ideally speaking. The older, "straw man" view cannot explain this fundamental fact of love.

What are some of the transformations of narcissism with adaptive potential? Kohut enumerates them as man's creativity, his ability to be empathic, his capacity to contemplate his own impermanence, his sense of humor, and his wisdom. And what is the relationship between romantic idealization of another and creativity? Kohut tells us that for the *average* individual, idealization, a transitional point in the development of narcissistic libido, survives only in states of being-in-love. The *gifted* individual idealizes—and despairs—about his work as well. That work, like a loved person, does settle down into possessing capacities of its very own—not simply the untransformed narcissistic wishes of the small child seeking out his or her double or twin self or dependence on the love-object as an idealized partner through whom one can live out one's life as one would wish it to be if it were perfect.

A Controversy between Critics

I shall now elaborate on the critical position taken by the more romantic Updike on the important relation between certain narcissistic elements in dyadic relationships and the creative process. De Rougemont, a Swiss theologian and essayist, has examined the classical medieval French myths underlying the plots of the love ballads produced by the troubadours of Languedoc. He announces that his purpose is "to describe the inescapable conflict in the West between passion and marriage." He analyzes the Tristan and Iseult legend to delineate the conflict between honorable marriage and unlimited, romantic, overidealizing passionate love.[1] He sees the occidental obsession with romantic love as the major cause of decline in civilized values. Such a love, if consummated, he says, opposes the realms of soul and spirit, and man's only escape from the temptations of the flesh is through asceticism and mystical "knowing." The religious function of the romantic ballads was to present a mythology of a fundamentally asexual, obstacle-ridden love that served at once to satisfy and check the "baser" demands of the populace. De Rougemont holds romanticism responsible for the "fact" that happy love has no history in Western literature. By his standards of happy love, he would most probably include Wotan's love for his daughter, Brünnhilde, in Wagner's *Die Walküre,* a form of affectionate companionship, which contrasts with the adulterous, incestuous love of the twins, Siegmund and Sieglinde, in the same opera. We, the audience, are persuaded by Wotan to forgive them their troubled love, and our capacity to forgive is reinforced by the disastrous outcomes to the human race resulting from their excesses. De Rougemont would argue that only the untroubled love is assimilable into Western cultural values, and thus, for him, it is unlikely that there can be a happy ending for the twins, Siegmund and Sieglinde, or for their psychologically equivalent characterizations of romantic love, Tristan and Isolde. Similar pronouncements would undoubtedly apply to other enthralled lovers, such as the at first rational, companionable Brünnhilde and Siegfried, the son of the incestuous twins in *Die Walküre,* whose love eventually becomes more tumultuous than any in the other operas of Wagner's Ring Cycle, *Siegfried* and *Götterdämmerung.* The theologian's negative evaluation of the romanticism in the Tristan myth springs from a similar source of judgment: the passionate connections through subterfuge and violation of the moral codes of the time are described as pathetic inventions to propagate a prototype of the "unattainable Lady," a prolongation of a state of mind—passion—whereby Eros is allied with Death and destroys marriage, social stability, and international peace. This love and death connection is the essence of the Liebestod mode of passionate love, a theme found not only in Wagner's music and libretti, but throughout diverse art forms in the Western world.

Updike contends that de Rougemont has been blinded to the essence of the romantic legends. Sexual passion *is* their essence. The sword between the sleeping Tristan and Iseult does not, as de Rougemont maintains, symbolize simply a civilization-preserving obstacle to ensure chastity, but also the parallel current of the lovers' sexual union. Updike adds that certain features that accompany Tristan and Iseult's narcissistic overidealization of each other provide the essential conditions upon which particular manifestations of creativity are honed. Happy, unobstructed love is the possibility that animates all romances. Updike explains de Rougemont's failure to recognize the possibility of passion coexisting with civilization as captivation by a rather Thomistic faith in and religious insistence on a total, uncompromising supremacy of the mind over instinct. Incestuous modes, de Rougemont says, must be kept from the masses: a man cannot marry an Iseult, "the woman . . . of his most intimate nostalgia, his mother." Lest all this Thomistic philosophy sound too much like the traditional psychoanalytic view regarding romantic passion as an illness, we must not forget that a man must come to terms with his fantasies of incest with mother and sister before he can be really free and happy in love: that, as Freud said (1905, 222), every finding in love is a refinding.

In keeping with Updike's interpretation and positive evaluation of romanticism, there are certain narcissistic modes of relating, touching on the process of inspired creativity, which need elaboration to illuminate the positive and creative values of these modes and the concomitant ego states they may reactivate in the overall context of object relatedness. We go back, then, to the earliest psychoanalytically understood developmental stages of life in our search for the normal roots of that passion that sometimes leads to the despair and misery that have captured the imaginations of poets and artists throughout eternity.

Early Ego States and Twin Narcissism

Twin narcissism is a term I borrow from de Rougemont, who uses it somewhat pejoratively to characterize the "being-in-love" aspects of Tristan and Iseult's unlimited passion: they are in love with their love.

It is best to delete the judgmental connotation and to define it simply as a more or less transient fusion state in which libidinal investment of the self is transferred to the object. This does not mean that other psychological states and functions may also be transferred as well. Self and object are loved as one because both share a love for a commonly esteemed activity, feeling state, or object. Generally speaking, and when there is a drive to enactment of a Liebestod fantasy, "the state of 'being in love' tends to draw imagery and sensations from these very early ego phases and aims towards fusion of self and non-self, even with an integrated and intact ego" (Bak 1973, 4). Twin narcissism is a term for fusion of self and object that is evocative of an early ego state common to infants, lovers, and some creative artists.

As Kohut's (1971) work has shown, the sharing of his own judgments about his work by projecting them onto the image of an empathic, sometimes adoring audience forms the narcissistic element in the core of the artist's fantasies, and constitutes a reenactment of the earliest being-in-love with his own creation, as the gleam in the father's eye. The creative urge is often triggered by a mutually empathic experience with an "other," and, subsequently, when creative activity requires solitude, the other may, in fantasy, be dismissed or beckoned at will, according to the requirements of the creative process unfolding. Mutual acknowledgment of the worth of the process and the product between creator and alter ego enhances feelings of self-regard that are indispensable for creativity. The twin narcissism of creativity, in short, has as its precursor that developmental stage characterized by, among other things, attachment to the transitional object (Winnicott 1953). The empathic bliss of symbiotic union with the "good enough" mother is partially renounced for the tentative but ecstatic glimpses of the burgeoning of one's separate, individuated development, and the expansion of the autonomous ego functions: function pleasure in being the "true self." To correlate this simplified description with Updike's ideas on romanticism, it may be said that the happy, passionate love of which he speaks has as its precursors a developmental stage and associated ego state that are also prototypical of creativity: the transitional-object developmental phase and its associated phenomena.

What are some of the critical relationships between twin narcissism and the creative process? Winnicott (1953) first described the transitional object as an essentially normal phenomenon arising from a particular need for support or "holding" during a period of marked growth involving early stages of individuation and separation from the mother. He emphasized that the transitional object is created by the child and loved in its own right as his creation, and is thus not simply a crutch to move from symbiosis to individuation.

Greenacre (1970, 343), too, lends support to the notion that the artist in a spell of creativity is recapturing the early ego state of when he was attached to a transitional object—the nostalgic juxtaposition of blissful reunion with the good mother and the ecstatic pleasure that accompanies the first autonomous steps away from her. Additionally, the prototypical artist had, as a child, experienced extreme sensitivity and inventiveness, especially at the point of change from what we may call single to twin omnipotence or narcissism.

Let us turn now to what Jacobson has to say about certain normal, yet vacillating mood states which seem to repeat the early ego states under consideration here. She offers the example of a young man who felt good after pleasant esteem-raising experiences with his girl friend and bad after unpleasant ones. He felt like a different person with a different relation to the world and the world in turn looked different to him. "It appears that an experience causes a change of mood only if it can bring about qualitative changes in the representations of the self and of the object world. . . . The moods transfer the qualities of the provocative experience to all objects and experiences; thus they impart a special coloring to the whole world and hence also to the self" (1971, 73, 80). This might well be applied to narcissism, creativity, and the perceptual style of the artist. The relation of mood to object love is well put by Jacobson, who said that a relieving "sweet sadness" may break through for people who have actually suffered a loss at the moment when they are achieving a libidinal recathexis of their lost objects and of pleasant memories relating to them. Kohut elaborates this relationship to encompass creativity and narcissism in saying that humor and creativity do not present a picture of grandiosity and elation, but of a quiet inner triumph admixed with melancholy. In a sense, every creative act is specifically based on the working through of depressive fantasies aiming at the reparation of early lost objects that one feels are damaged.

Twin Narcissism and Creativity

Twin narcissism, as conceptualized here, is not simply based on Shakespearean mockery of what narcissistic fools imagine exists between themselves, when in love. It is a valuable developmental milestone implying high-level transformations of primary narcissism. Greenacre (1957, 483) speaks of the way Kris (1952), in his well-known psychoanalytic work on art and creativity, facilitated her creativity, and we are all familiar with how Freud was, for a time, nourished by his relationship with his "self-created object," Fliess (Schur 1972). So, returning to the critics' controversy, I shall consider a particular aspect of creativity which, though it may occasionally involve a transient surfacing of regressive components, is, like Kris's regression in the service of the ego, essentially nonregressive.[2] This view, like Kohut's, regards creativity as a healthy, adaptive transformation of certain vagaries of narcissism.

The spectrum of narcissism is particularly well-illustrated by the transitional object fetish contrast and, on another level, by the contrast between Updike and de Rougemont in their interpretations of the Tristan myth. De Rougemont's proclamation that love takes the form of romantic inaccessibility logically leads to his negative ideas about passionate love feeding on denial and to his contention that the love myth as expressed in the romantic troubadour songs states that avidity for possession is more delightful than possession itself: "to possess her is to lose her." Freud (1914) characterized "the purest and truest" feminine type as narcissistic. The condition of women loving themselves with an intensity comparable to that of the man's love for them, and of one person's narcissism having a great attraction for another, is not solely regressive. Mutually being "in thrall" may precede and persist contrapuntally with object love, sustaining it over time. In fact, the two modes of loving coexist precisely because they radiate from narcissistic and object-libidinal lines of development respectively. The posthumously published paper, "The Dual Orientation of Narcissism," by Lou Andreas-Salomé (1922) considers some of the positive aspects of twin or shared narcissism, especially as they affect the creative process. According to Andreas-Salomé, the creative direction of narcissism, aided by the ego, contains vitally important residues of the primal, unambivalent union of mother and child, implying an object relation from the start. That Andreas-Salomé was, on the other hand, greatly influenced by the elements de Rougemont pejoratively attributes to romanticism is evident in her Liebestod-like ideas about narcissistic love in its other orientation, ending in the *annihilation* of the object: "With the progress of ecstatic love, as the object is more and more unreservedly magnified, the more does the object behind its manifest symbolic form remain undernourished and devitalized. The more fiery the fanaticism of love, the more cooling is the effort of its distortions— until climactically fire and frost are one" (1922, 12–13). She contrasts such narcissistically self-destructive forms of passionate love with a narcissistically productive, friendly love of two who "are at one in God, or only in collecting or going fishing." In both types of love, there is a narcissistic overestimation of the love object. But here,

> The heart of the matter is this: whatever love, honor, even transfiguration the friend may attain in our eyes comes from this "third," which is able to forge bonds stronger than those of personal erotism. Detached from goal of sexual possession, everything imaginable seems attainable to the libido thus elaborated, and with the sublimation of the most archaic autoerotism it arrives at a confusion of self and world experienced à deux. In exchange for the narrow scope imposed by the genital love of a particular person, the broadest compass is permitted to narcissism that has successfully developed outside the range of genitality. (13–14)

This particular quotation implies that the narcissistic self-other dyad or creativity "à deux" requires sublimation, which, in turn, depends on the eternal promise of reunion with the primary maternal object. Symbiosis, fusion, and merger, then, as normal developmental states may lead not only to normal but to creative developmental outcomes, despite the potential for any normal development to go awry into the pathological.

The relation between external sources of self-esteem regulation and the autonomous function of the ego as it is directed toward creativity is set forth compassionately:

> No autonomous ethical stand can exist without the promise of the mother's warm embrace. Everything that we call sublimation depends on this possibility—that we can retain something of that lost intimacy of the libidinal attitude toward even the most abstract and the least personal things. This alone prompts the process whereby "sexual energy, all or in part, abandons the sexual route and is drawn to other goals." (18)

This paper, written in 1921, predates theoretical developments in ego psychology, object relations, and child development, and would appear to reflect both Updike's and de Rougemont's perspectives by virtue of the emphasis on the dual orientation. In discussing the essential duality of narcissism, Andreas-Salomé stresses two elements. One has to do with self-love, which when excessive annihilates both self and object—the Liebestod—a validation of de Rougemont's position. The other has to do with the "persistent feeling of identification with the totality," or fusion with an Other and with shared values, ideals, and loves, which she says underlie "narcissistic transformation to artistic creativity" (5), an element that validates Updike's and Kohut's position. As Kohut notes on twin narcissism, "The creative individual, whether in art or science, is less psychologically separated from his surroundings than the noncreative one; the 'I-you' barrier is not as clearly defined" (1966, 259).

Updike, like Andreas-Salomé and Kohut, rejects the negative view of idealization of the love-object, and of the exclusively narcissistic state that some would hold that the Tristan myth implies, whereas de Rougemont clearly attributes pejorative values to such idealization: "Tristan and Iseult are, de Rougemont concludes, in love not with one another, but with love itself, with their own *being* in love; their unhappiness thus originates in a false reciprocity which disguises a twin narcissism" (Updike 1963, 90). Updike also rejects de

Rougemont's gloomy pronouncements on romanticism, celebrating instead the positive and affirmative aspects not only of the myth but of the Tristan-and-Iseult mode of loving, or the creative aspects of twin narcissism that may not only survive but even flourish within the range of genitality.

Before I expand on the flourishing of twin narcissism in the normal realm of psychic functioning, I would like to turn to another example in Wagner's *Die Walküre*. Twin narcissism, in this instance a literal twin narcissism, could be said to have survived within the range of genitality as we look further into the way Wagner's libretto (Skelton-Porter version in John 1983) depicts the incestuous union of the Wälsung twins, Siegmund and Sieglinde, which he himself, in an 1851 letter to Liszt, described as "wonderful yet disastrous" (John 1983). Although their love was doomed and ill-fated (their parents had been given a magic apple to eat, a symbol, like the love potion in *Tristan und Isolde,* of fatal attractions and outcomes), as expressed in a disastrous Liebestod scene (to be described, later, in context), they did bear a son, Siegfried. It must be more than mere coincidence that the lovers are twins, for the twinship is a wonderful metaphor to express the psychological aspects of their narcissistically based love affair, in which, over and above Wagner's explicit artistic aims, they serve as self-objects for one another. In their encounter, the first after having been separated since earliest childhood when their home was burnt to the ground and their mother died, they fall in love immediately upon sighting one another. The libretto is replete, as we shall soon see, with references to eyes, glances, looking, and mirroring gazing, capturing, in its text, the essence of the relation between twin narcissism and romantic love discussed in this chapter. Although they respond at first as though they were strangers, recognition and familiarity come almost immediately and the sense of always having known not only each other but that they were to be "star-crossed lovers" proceeds with amazing rapidity. Furthermore, the two halves of the musical passage expressing the couple's falling-in-love are heard in reverse order, suggesting a musical rendering of a visual mirror image, once again the metaphor, this time in musical language, for twin narcissism. With this musical mirroring background, the pair gaze at each other in an unspoken affirmation of their love: "his eyes fix themselves with calm and steady sympathy on Sieglinde. Slowly, she raises her eyes again to his. They gaze into one another's eyes, during a long silence, with an expression of the deepest emotion" (John 1984, 57). The libretto continues as Siegmund turns his eyes to Sieglinde and observes her sympathetic glance:

> Then she turns her eyes on Siegmund so as to meet his gaze, which he keeps unceasingly fixed on her. . . . On the steps she turns once more, looks yearningly at Siegmund, and indicates with her eyes, persistently and with eloquent earnestness a particular spot on the oak-tree's trunk to guide him to the sword which she hopes will save his life. (61)

She throws her arms around his neck, enraptured, and gazes closely into his face, as recognition begins to dawn, because of all this mirroring, that they are twin brother and sister. The following passage is meant to convey that one or both has recognized their blood connection as the Wälsung twins, as memories of their joint past are retrieved:

> And your gleaming glance
> I've seen it before:
> The stranger in grey
> gazed on me thus
> when he came to console my grief. (66)

All of this gazing is not simply a function of their retrieving memories and recognizing themselves in each other, but reflects a twinship fantasy of romantic love, which in this instance happens to be an echo of their biological reality. In Sieglinde's fantasy, she has loved this man all her life and had long ago actually given him the name, Siegmund (his real name happened to be Friedmunde) to match her own. I return now to an understanding of how even these romantic fantasies, which Wagner so brilliantly transformed into his great art, have adaptive aspects along with their depiction of doom, gloom, and fatal attraction.

The adaptive aspects of transformed narcissism parallel object constancy and genitally mature heterosexuality. Being-in-love thereby might be regarded as a transiently revived "state," and loving as a structuralized, constant mode of object relatedness. Updike concludes his critique of de Rougemont on narcissism:

> Again, the charge of narcissism that de Rougemont levels against lovers of the Tristan-and-Iseult type seems dubiously fair, for, as Freud in his essay on narcissism points out, "the human being has originally two sexual objects: himself and the woman who tends him": That is, in feeling or making love, the lover shares in the glorification—the "overestimation"—of the beloved; his own person becomes itself lovely. These selfish and altruistic threads in these emotions are surely inseparable. (94)

It is worth recalling Freud's actual words:

> We have, however, not concluded that human beings are divided into two sharply differentiated groups, according as their object-choice conforms to the anaclitic or to the narcissistic type; we assume rather that both kinds of object-choice are open to each individual, though he may show a preference for one or the other. We say that a human being has originally two sexual objects—himself and the woman who nurses him—and in doing so we are postulating a primary narcissism in everyone. (1914, 88)

Thus Freud, though referring to primary infantile objects rather than to later self-created ones, nonetheless laid the groundwork from which Kohut later developed his thesis. As for the relationship between narcissism and object love, Freud said, "it seems very evident that another person's narcissism has a great attraction for those who have renounced part of their own narcissism and are in search of object-love" (1914, 89).

Stimulus Hunger and Romanticism

The recent conceptual delineation between the ego and the self bypasses easily the arguments about positioning creativity somewhere between asceticism and self-abnegation, on the one hand, and gratification and self-indulgence on the other. The internalization of self-esteem touches on both the object-libidinal and narcissistic lines of development. When these are regarded as parallel rather than mutually exclusive, it makes pointless the tired debates about whether creativity thrives better on starvation or satiation. The psychoanalyst, the poet, and, of course, the lover, may appreciate the effects on the creative process of stimulus hunger, stimulus seeking, and stimulus manipulation.

Illusion-formation during the transitional-object phase bears a critically important kinship to the overvaluation, the overidealization of the self-created love-object, a normal narcissistic component of attachment behavior generally, and of the romantic prelude to constancy and mutuality in object relations. Greenacre has suggested that such illusion formation is particularly related to the creative process in sensitive and particularly gifted individuals. With the onset of walking, the child's perception changes in the direction of an obligatory enrichment of the range and combinations of sensory ingredients and therefore an increased exploratory capacity:

> My point here is that the introjective-projective relation to the outside *is by no means an inability to distinguish the boundary between the self and the other, or even a simple mirroring*. . . . This flexibly changing interplay of sensorimotor responses to the external object must furnish the possibility for myriad illusions to occur, before the exploratory experiences have been repeated sufficiently that a central core of reliable expectancy has formed, *permitting the perceived object gradually to settle down to a recognizable entity or identity of its own.* (Greenacre 1970, 347 [italics added])

Illusions, idealizations, and object constancy coexist in the best of all possible loves. Here we see that the merging, fusing processes of both introjective and projective mechanisms have an adaptive potential. We have already come a long way from what has traditionally been regarded as only the most primitive defense mechanisms, for they may, in good enough situations, form the basis for empathy. At such times, they may be regarded as highly adaptive precursors to both creativity and object relations—an idealization of self-created work and self-created objects as well as a respect for that otherness which is not self-created, but aided and abetted by the narcissistic capacities for self-creation and its transformations.

We are familiar with that quality of narcissism which, if not rein-forced or mirrored by someone, produces a lowering of self-esteem that stimulates rage and depression of such intensity and durability as to be ended only and temporarily by the next external mirroring of the "ideal self." Freud described the relationship between self-regard and object-cathexes by stating,

> Loving, in itself, in so far as it involves longing and deprivation, lowers self-regard; whereas being loved, having one's love returned, and pos-sessing the loved object, raises it once more. . . . The return of the object-libido to the ego and its transformation into narcissism repre-sents, as it were, a happy love once more; and, on the other hand, it is also true that a real happy love corresponds to the primal condition in which object libido and ego-libido cannot be distinguished. (1914, 99–100)

Whether from the mother, the lover, the psychoanalyst, or fortuitous and serendipitous life circumstances, the *constant* flow of external sources of narcissistic supplies becomes superfluous following the developmental process of internalization, leading to object con-stancy—the stable internalized image of a good object relationship, and of course, the internalization of self-regard. Yet, clearly, certain longings do not disappear even with a life of reasonable instinctual satisfaction, good internalized object relationships, and routine work productivity. To work in a better-than-pedestrian manner, there must be some glorification, adoration, idealization of people and products, while the healthy grasp of reality's more severe limits are temporarily suspended. Andreas-Salomé's "no autonomous . . . stand can exist without the promise of the mother's warm embrace" fittingly applies. Updike speaks of how "eternal" relationships hope to preserve origi-nal passion and thereby creativity, contrasting the position that the more abstinent modes of loving are more qualified to achieve this end with his own belief that sexually passionate love may be equally effective. He faults de Rougemont's interpretation of such well-known stories as Racine's *Phèdre* and Madame de Lafayette's *La Princesse de Clèves,* which would have them representative of the more abstinent modes.

We must question Updike's endorsement of the verdict delivered by the Comtesse de Champagne in 1174 when the favorite question about courtly love proposed in a Court of Love was, "Can true love exist between married people?" The Comtesse stated and affirmed by the tenor of those present that love could not extend its rights over two married persons. Updike explains the extramarital prerequisite for creative narcissism in the Tristan-and-Iseult mode of loving as an escape valve from the hazards of too much biological contentment. A less extreme, less literal approach is required to reconcile the demands of a long-term routinized relationship with the romantic-erotic conditions required for creativity, and Updike himself is onto it, linking the essential condition to the quest for variety in the stimulus or love-object. This approach correctly bypasses sociological considerations and brings to mind Schachtel's (1959) views about man's craving for stimulation in infinite variety. Freud, Schachtel, Greenacre, and others regard the quest for change as an important aspect of love not related to "varietism" or other pathological variations with morally dubious connotations. Updike ties the quest for variety to the mechanism of sublimation: "The body's chronic appetites can be satisfied by repetition, but, merged with the mind's quest for new knowledge, they become insatiable. Fickleness is the price we pay for individualizing one another" (102). Similarly, Jacobson (1971) reminds us that Goethe's statement, "nothing is harder to bear than a series of good days," evidently was meant to convey that "in a prolonged specific pleasure experience we become gradually aware of unpleasure feelings indicating the 'urge for a change' in the situation" (27). Ethel Person's (1989) recent work on "love attacks" amongst stable, yes, married lovers, gets at this truth in a novel and creative way.

Greenacre provides a conceptual bridge between love, stimulus hunger, and creativity. She, like Bergman and Escalona (1949) acknowledges that, in the specially gifted person there may be an unusual sensitivity to all sensory and kinesthetic stimulations. The second year of life

> is a time of infinite stimulating surprises, which are invigorating under good-enough mothering conditions but may be desperately frightening

in states of distress and deprivation. The transitional object based on the good mother-me dyad relationship when the distinction between the mother and the infant is not clearly defined, can then carry multiple reassuring illusions, and in this way consolidate the stable perceptive appreciation of many new objects both animate and inanimate. It is then a period of burgeoning discovery, and its conquests have such an impact as to open up the surrounding but unexpected universe. (351)

Greenacre has thus helped put to rest the near eternal debate about the relative importance of tension reduction versus stimulus seeking. The principles do not in any way contradict one another viewed in the context of development of the total personality, and especially of the regulatory principle of homeostasis. Contemporary psychoanalysis would perhaps view normal gratification of instinctual needs as a necessary but not sufficient condition for maximum productivity and creativity. Perhaps the sufficient conditions are supplemented by some kind of sublimated living out of the Tristan myth.

Kohut (1971) has dignified narcissistic transference relationships. With special reference to creativity, he notes that the solving of an intellectual or aesthetic problem always leads to a feeling of narcissistic pleasure. Empathic, merging contact, quite outside the realm of pathology may also be observed as

> when certain creative personalities appear to require a specific relationship during periods of intense creativity. This need is especially strong when discoveries lead the creative mind into lonely areas that had not previously been explored by others . . . . we are dealing either with the expansion of an active, creative self, or . . . with the wish to obtain strength from an idealized object (idealizing transference), but not predominantly with the revival of a figure from the past which is cathected with object libido. (316–17)

It is indeed beginning to sound, paradoxically perhaps, as though the grand passions of romantic love are not primarily involved with sexual libidinal gratification, though of course they are part of it. If anything, their unique accent is on the nonsexual, so the drive aspects of psychoanalysis, while playing their part as always, may not warrant a central part of the stage in our understanding of the normal and pathological situations which are the main subject matter of this book.

Summary

Although psychoanalysts, until very recently, have been unable to explain the nature of love, they have dealt with the related topics of narcissistic and object libido: that is, sexual feelings directed either toward the self or toward others. This chapter has attempted to expand the more well-accepted notions into a general notion of love, death, and romanticism, drawing from the arts where psychoanalysis has insufficiently explored.

Certain transformations of narcissism and idealization contribute to the creative process. A consideration of some forms and transformations of narcissism discussed by Kohut is offered here as applied to the romanticism of the Tristan and Iseult legend, with specific reference to a revival of early ego states. Andreas-Salomé's views on the dual orientation of narcissism are presented as a particularly helpful way of reconciling the apparent contradiction between the "new" and "old" views of narcissism.

This chapter notably omits reference to the work of Margaret Mahler and her co-workers (1975) in understanding related phenomena, although the connection between romantic love and difficulties in separating from the other has been addressed. Preferring death to an unthinkable life without the partner does indeed sound not just like a revival of an early ego state, but like a form of pathological regression involving loss of self-boundaries. From that point of view, one would need to think of clinical analysis as promoting an advance from the Liebestod to true, individuated object love. But, as we shall see, it is not so easy to distinguish residues of the normal from pathological developments in the Liebestod, and Mahler's work should prove useful in helping us make those distinctions. Chapter 2 attempts to do justice to her important contributions.

Two

On Love, Dying, and Liebestod Fantasies

"My lords, if you would hear a high tale of love and death," starts the troubadour version of the legend of Tristan and Iseult, "how to their full joy, but to their sorrow also, they loved each other, and how at last they died of that love together upon one day; she by him and he by her." The love-death, or Liebestod motif of the story condenses multiple fantasies and invites a general psychoanalytic study of the legend's meaning. In particular, one might aim to illuminate the phenomenon of being-in-love and its various outcomes, only one of which is the relatively unexplored but clinically important yearning to die together. Of all the themes of this legend, the Liebestod motif or the theme of fatal love is the most powerful. It is also a major class of fantasy of love and death in both art and life. I shall first summarize the Celtic legend's plot:

Tristan is born in misfortune. His father has just died and his mother dies in childbirth. He is raised by King Mark of Cornwall, his loving and beloved uncle, and performs feats of prowess at an early age, continuing his heroics throughout life. At puberty, he kills the giant Morholt of Ireland, who had been exacting an unending tribute of local maidens and youths, and becomes mortally wounded. This giant was the brother of the queen of Ireland and the queen's daughter,

Iseult, nurses Tristan back to health with a magic cure, not knowing he was her uncle's slayer. Some years later, Tristan is sent by King Mark to bring back Iseult to be Mark's bride. After killing a dragon to save the populace, he is wounded once more, and once more Iseult nurses him back to health, this time learning that he is her uncle's killer, whereupon she threatens to kill him but decides to spare him once she learns of his mission to bring her back as his uncle's bride. On sailing for Cornwall, Tristan and Iseult are tricked into drinking the magic love potion whose effect, although they do not know it, is to render them forever in love with one another and to commit them to a fate from which they can never escape, *for they have drunk their destruction and death*. One cannot live or die without the other. They consummate their love. Notwithstanding his betrayal of his uncle, Tristan delivers Iseult to Mark, and the King and Iseult wed.

Tristan and Iseult remain lovers, and successfully contrive to meet secretly for some time, until the felon barons, Tristan's rivals for Mark's favor and love, report the adultery to the King. For a while, the lovers trick Mark into believing their innocence, but the felons finally confront Mark with incontrovertible evidence of their adultery. Mark hands Iseult over to one hundred lepers, and sentences Tristan to the stake. Through heroic efforts, Tristan escapes his fate and rescues Iseult from hers, and for three years they lead a harsh and hard life as exiles in the forest. At the end of that time, Mark comes upon them while they are asleep, and deceives himself that they are innocent.

According to most versions of the legend, it is at this point that the potency of the love potion wears off. Tristan repents, and Iseult wishes she were queen again. Tristan surrenders Iseult to Mark, who promises forgiveness. Now separated, the lovers pledge to reunite whenever either shall wish it, and so they part and come together, overcoming obstacles of the felon barons and their own making alike. Subterfuges, disguises, and ordeals abound. Finally, after a self-created agony that Iseult no longer loves him, Tristan marries another Iseult. Wounded in a final grand feat, Tristan is about to die and sends for Iseult his lover, for only she has the power to save his life, if the ship which brings her hoists a white sail. Tristan's wife, Iseult, tormented by jealousy, tells him the boat's sail is black, and Tristan dies. Iseult lands, lies down beside her dead lover, and clasps him close. Then she dies too. (See figure 1.)

Figure 1. Iseult lands, lies down beside her dead lover, and clasps him close. Then she dies too. (Richard Wagner, *Isolde's Liebestod.* Postcard, Music Division, The New York Public Library for the Performing Arts, Astor, Lenox, and Tilden Foundations. ICON Opera File, *Tristan und Isolde,* #17.)

Most psychoanalysts today would see this legend as a vehicle to express certain vicissitudes of being-in-love. I shall rely, therefore, on the legend to generate hypotheses and formulations about the psychology of love, and will not attempt a psychoanalysis of the work as a piece of literature. Since a major purpose of this book is to study both normal and pathological aspects of the phenomena in question, I shall offer an approach to the psychology of love, embodied in the Liebestod, which avoids polarization—for example, of loving versus being-in-love; of symbiotic versus oedipal genesis; of repressed ego state versus ego capacity—which has characterized much of the psychoanalytic literature on that subject.

Current works (Bak 1973, Bergmann 1971, Gediman 1975, 1981) have looked upon being-in-love as a "state," derived primarily from the earliest impressions and memory traces of the blissful symbiotic stage, the stage that precedes a sense of separateness from the mother. It would not be at all difficult to deduce from the legend, as summarized above, that yearning for the lost bliss, fusion, and merging feelings of symbiosis underlies the movement of the lovers toward eternal reunion through death together. However, to reduce the quest for being-in-love to revived symbiotic longings alone is to commit the "genetic fallacy," whereby to explain all facets of complex adult patterns of love as derivatives of impressions of the earliest infantile state and related universal fantasies is to explain nothing at all. I propose to illuminate the nature of loving and being-in-love by analyzing the multiple fantasies expressed in the legend of Tristan and Iseult and in the other legends informing the plots of Richard Wagner's Ring Cycle, with particular emphasis on the Liebestod motif. In the course of this discussion, I shall also take up a number of themes that occupy a place in any psychoanalytic discussion of passionate love: object loss and yearning to die together; longing for reunion through death; oedipal longings in the Liebestod; sadomasochism; conflicts over merger and autonomy; double and mass suicide; and death and rebirth.

The version of the Tristan legend just summarized, on which my inferences will be based, is in fact a composite of five, separately authored, tellings.[1] Therefore, it would not be correct to offer strictly genetic hypotheses as if we were looking at an actual case study. This legend stands as a statement about some important facets of human existence. A thorough understanding of this statement requires some imaginative speculation about critical events in the life of the legendary Tristan in order to generalize on an expanded psychology of love. I focus primarily on Tristan's and not Iseult's life because the legend provides us only with a vague, sketchy notion of the woman, whereas it approaches more of a three-dimensional characterization of the man. Some believe the sketchy depiction of Iseult reflects the secondary status of women at the time of the legend's evolution. Others feel the sketchiness is consistent with the characterological remoteness in the romantic idealization of the prototype of the unattainable lady, the femme fatale, which typified the romantic view of women. The reasons, whatever they may be, are not the main emphasis of this book.

Yearning to Die Together

Yearning to refind the early, lost feelings of the bliss of merger is one critically important motive that underlies the quest for eternal reunion in much of romantic love (see Person 1989 and Bergmann 1987). Chaste and lusty double-death motifs reflect these longings, and were so characteristic in medieval song and legend that "no stylish medieval household was complete without an effigy of Pyramus and Thisbe or Tristan and Isolt . . . Two other medievals, Francesca and Paolo, slain as they slipped into sin, made it to the Renaissance" (Binion 1993, 46). So too did the Liebestod yearnings for merger of Petrarch and Laura, and of Dante and Beatrice (see figure 2). Of course, there is also much evidence in the songs of the medieval troubadours, Renaissance painting, Elizabethan poems, and nineteenth-century romantic literature for the merger of the Liebestod. Binion, well aware of the suggestion of merger and reunion throughout the ages, is most interested in its nineteenth century romantic transformations. He refers to Turgenev's 1882 novel, *Clara Miltitch,* in which Arátoff, having dreamed he was dead beside his dead beloved Clara, "felt himself in her power until he perished in fevered

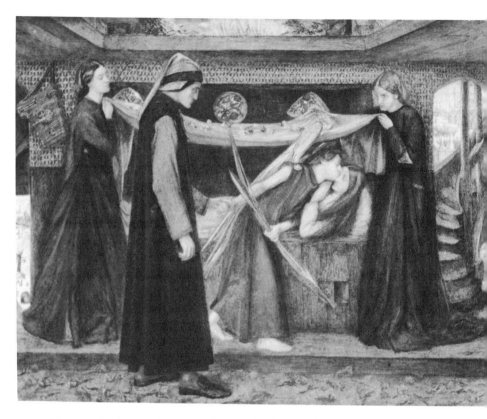

Figure 2. A nineteenth-century Pre-Raphaelite rendering of the Liebestod yearning for reunion and merger. (Dante Gabriel Rossetti, *Dante's Dream at the Time of the Death of Beatrice* [1856]. Tate Gallery/Art Resource, New York.)

bliss at the thought of rejoining her" (14). Similarly, in Flaubert's 1874 *La Tentation de Saint Antoine,* Anthony says, as he imagines himself martyred along with his beloved Ammonaria, "Our pain would have mingled, our souls would have mixed" (Binion 1993, 17). Thus, the prototypical Tristan legend of yearning for reunion by dying together persisted throughout the ages.

Broadly speaking, lovers yearn to die together for two related reasons: one is to express the wish for a "good" death via symbiotic union and merger, and the other is to ward off and master the possibilities of a "bad" death and all that the latter may signify, symbolically.

"Good" and "Bad" Deaths in Fatal Attractions

Tristan's eternal longing for the love-death was first and foremost fashioned from the death of his parents, his father's before he was born, his mother's while giving birth to him:

> He who begot me died, she dying gave me birth.
> . . . .
> what fate for me was chosen,
> when then my mother bore me,
> what fate for me?
> The olden ditty once more tells me:
> 'tis yearning and dying! . . .
> Yearning now calls
> for death's repose. (Quoted in de Rougemont 1956, 50)

Early parental deaths often do provide the trauma that people try to master throughout life via passionate attachments. In Wagner's *Tristan und Isolde,* the leitmotif music of the love duet conveys the twin nostalgia for oneness in the ecstatic release of dying together. Tristan's parents both died by the time he was born, and this double loss might predispose any child to develop fantasies of atonement, or regaining lost parents, and of reunion through death. In fact, the troubadour version holds these deaths responsible for Tristan's chronic "yearning for dying." The parents' deaths may be the trauma that Tristan is trying to master throughout his life, providing the context out of which the Liebestod leitmotif develops. Here we note a legendary representation of what real life is all about even when the parents do not actually die: the yearnings and attempts to refind the lost idealized parental image of each developmental phase.

In two other Wagner operas, *Die Walküre* and *Siegfried,* musical Liebestod motifs mark the death of Siegfried's parents, the twins Siegmund and Sieglinde, in the midst of their passionate, adulterous, and incestuous love affair. Twin fantasies are importantly involved in Wagner's renditions of yearning and dying and, as noted in the previous chapter, one observes both the pathological and the not-so-pathological aspects of twin narcissism in many instances of passionate love. Wagner's *Walküre* lyrics poignantly inform the background of death and destruction about which Siegmund reminisces practically at the very moment he sets eyes on Sieglinde:

> His two children were twins—
> my unhappy sister and I
>   Both mother and sister
>   were lost—
>   my mother killed
>   and my sister borne off
>   . . . .
> and found our home laid waste
>   a heap of ash
>   was all that was left;
>   a stump where once
>   an oak tree had stood;
>   the corpse of my mother
>   lay at my feet;
>   all trace of my sister
>   was lost in smoke. (John 1983, 58)

In *Siegfried,* the sequel to *Die Walküre,* the banished Sieglinde gives birth to Siegfried in the wilderness and then dies. Like Tristan, Siegfried, the child who has suffered the deaths of both parents, is raised by men not women. Siegfried was raised by the dwarf Mime, whom he hated, just as Tristan was raised mainly by the dwarf, Kurwenal. Being thus reared by men who are held in contempt, when compared with their idealized biological fathers whom they never knew, may also contribute in some important way to the passionate yearnings for a woman, which transform into the yearning for death and reunion. Siegfried repeatedly asks the dwarf Mime, "Wer ist mir Vater und Mutter?" (Who are my father and mother?). Mime, who does not even know the name of Siegfried's father, responds,

> A child stirred in her body
> sadly she gave it birth
> That birth was cruel and hard
> I helped as best I could
> Great was her pain! She died.
> But Siegfried, you were born. (John 1984, 71)

The search for the lost parents who have died, the wish to refind them, appears to be basic, once again, to love fueled by Liebestod fantasies. An important theme in the opera, *Siegfried,* is the young boy's fearless wish to avenge the death of his father, Siegmund, which he does by reforging the sword, Notung, that had killed Siegmund. Siegfried's feats, like Tristan's, have the quality of "swashbuckling" omnipotence, as he goes on to kill the giant, Fafner, with the magic sword, finally retrieving the valuable Rhinegold in the form of the Ring and the Tarnhelm. Siegfried, who never had a serious oedipal rival, then kills his "foster" father, Mime, who had planned to kill Siegfried in order to get possession of the magically protective Ring for himself. That fearlessness, too, appears connected to his lack of a parental, maternal figure, for it is only later in young adulthood, when he sets eyes on the sleeping Brünnhilde, whom he first mistakes for his dead mother, that Siegfried experiences fear for the first time. That newly developed angst, a belated amalgam of oedipal and existential anxieties, appears to be a condition motivating the Liebestod. The last act of the opera ends with a love duet between Siegfried and Brünnhilde, a reminder that Siegfried is a love-child of a Liebestod romance and not the offspring of a single dwarf. The plot elements and Wagner's musical motifs herald Siegfried's fate of the Liebestod that occurs at the opera's finale. Before falling desperately in love with Brünnhilde, Siegfried has known and had commerce only with

animals, with one dwarf whom he regarded as a pathetic and con-
temptible father surrogate, with giants, and with Gods. As he falls in
love with a woman and experiences fear, he becomes a feeling and
thinking member of the human race. It is as though being smitten
with love leads to the knowledge of death, which then leads both
to oedipal anxieties and to that existential angst that characterizes
humankind, in parallel manner to Christ's incarnation (to be discussed in a later chapter of this book, in connection with resurrection
fantasies), rendering him in touch with human misery and suffering.
Romantic love, then, in this context is to be regarded as human and
normal by virtue of its very connection with knowledge of death and
its ensuing existential anxieties. It is not only a pathological aberration characterized by emotional excess and fatal outcomes.

This existential angst is missing from the lives of both Tristan and
Siegfried until they meet their respective "femme fatales," and it is
then that they are both tormented by the anguish that comes from
yearning for both love and death. The absence of the mother, together with the death of their idealized fathers and the being raised
by dwarfs whom both Tristan and Siegfried hold in contempt, leading
to an absence of oedipal triangulation and rivalry during the forma-
tive years, is a sine qua non of Liebestod yearnings. If these men were
real and not fictional characters, we would conclude confidently
that such early histories of loss of the parents, and the subsequent
childrearing conditions predisposed them to the syndrome of fearless,
omnipotent heroics in the name of the father in an attempt both to
identify with him as ideal, and to reunite with him, culminating in
the passionate Liebestod with its accompanying wish to reunite, as
well, with the dead mother.

Turning now, from Wagner's opera, *Tristan und Isolde,* to the
Celtic legend of Tristan and Iseult, we note that Tristan, like all Celtic
youths, was raised only by men—by King Mark and by other father
surrogates—and sheltered from women. He was trained to perform
magnificent feats, and then, at puberty, was knighted by Mark for his
many heroic deeds and miraculous rescues and escapes from death
which were to continue through his life. These feats would eventually
earn him the right to marry. Tristan was revered prematurely as

a lord, not merely loved as a son by his father surrogates. This aggrandizement would, in a child, tend to predispose to precocity and to a narcissistic sense of entitlement, which is implied in Tristan's grand and grandiose heroics throughout the legend. Tristan's passion to assert his prowess in moments of peril always involves suffering and courting of death, the "beloved pain of the troubadours," which is perhaps masochistic, perhaps counterphobic, and most likely a forerunner of the love-death through attempts at active mastery of the passively feared death. Here again, his life may be understood to be a repetitive reliving of the trauma of loss in order to master it.

It is always of interest to know what events in the life of an artist might have provided the psychological motivation for creating those themes that repeatedly appear in the work of that artist. Psychoanalysts use what they refer to as the "pathographic method" of investigation when they try to discern events in the real and psychic life of the artist that had such influence. Once these events are known, they then aid in interpreting the meaning of aspects of a work of art which are then subjected to a thematic analysis (see Spitz 1985). What might have occurred in Wagner's life that drew him so magnetically to themes of love and death in his magnificent works? As was the case for his heroes and heroines, he, too, suffered the death of a parent in childhood. At the age of eight, his father died, and biographical studies (Millington 1984; Newman 1924; von Westernhagen 1978) provide plentiful evidence for the impact of that loss on his psyche and on his entire life, including his operatic works. On the basis of a pathographic approach to analyzing the facts laid out by Wagner's biographers, the following interpretation is justified.

Wagner, in his artistic rendition of a story with a predominant theme of a love-death between twins, presents us with his versions of the important fantasy of the twin, double, or Doppelganger (see Freud 1919) in which the one to whom one is "fatally" attracted also acts to ward off death. One person may seek his or her own death to achieve eternal reunion with the loved one as second self, or "self-object," and this seeking of the "good death" paradoxically wards off the devil, or "bad" death, as representing irrevocable loss. A fruitful, pathographic interpretation of Wagner's personal motives for repeating the Liebestod leitmotif in his art, which was so heavily laden with musical and narrative themes of love and death, is that they reflected the artist's own repetitive expression of the wish for reunion with *his* lost, dead father. Derrick Puffet (John 1984) notes parallels in the lives of the fictional Siegfried and the fictional Tristan, who I believe must reflect important events in the life of their creator, who chose these particular legendary and mythical characters to express his own emotional truths. Not only were both raised by dwarfs, as noted above, but both had important relations as surrogate sons of powerful men: Tristan with King Mark and Siegfried with the God, Wotan, who appears in the opera *Siegfried,* as the Wanderer. Psychoanalysis yet awaits a systematic and comprehensive pathographic study of Wagner's musical masterpieces that fully uses the plethora of documented biographical information at its disposal to enable deeper interpretations relating his life to his art. While such an endeavor is beyond the scope of this present book, I shall try to provide typical examples of the connections between the artist's art and the artist's life. One example is that at the time of writing *Siegfried,* Wagner's life was very connected to King Ludwig of Bavaria, more about which will be said later. He had also married Cosima von Bülow. The last act of *Siegfried,* where the hero meets Brünnhilde and where Liebestod themes emerge, was written years after the first two acts. Between the years 1857, when the opera *Siegfried* was begun, and 1869 when Act III was written, Wagner had written *Tristan und Isolde,* and those who know both operas cannot help being reminded of the Tristan Liebestod when encountering Siegfried's similar Liebestod yearnings for love and death. For now, though, I return to a reconsideration of twin narcissism and death yearnings.

Liebestod Yearnings and Twin Narcissism

The twin fantasy, the merger fantasy, or the fantasy of the double relates to an aspect of being-in-love that seems to characterize the Tristan-and-Iseult type of relationship: each is a "selfobject" (Kohut 1971) for the other. De Rougemont (1956) noted that each loves the other from the "standpoint of the self." From this observation, he reasoned that their unhappiness originated in a false reciprocity which disguises a "twin narcissism." Joseph (1959) tells us that twin fantasies may arise to deal with the fear that either of two in a critical relationship might perish, and may be an outgrowth of pathological identifications and ambivalence. Indeed, Tristan and Iseult's state of unhappiness is doubled, for they both have married people they do not love, and they thereby achieve a greater sense of communion. Their joint misery and despair heightens the twinship aspect of their love.

I elaborated the twin narcissism concept in chapter 1 where, although I borrowed the term from de Rougemont's scholarly work on love in the Western world, I questioned his pejorative or exclusively narcissistic characterization of Tristan and Iseult's unlimited passion and his assertion that they are in love *only* with their love. Self and object often may be loved as one when both individuals share a love for a commonly esteemed activity, feeling state, or object. In that chapter, I also spoke of the frequent coexistence in one and the same individual of the twin narcissism of *being-in-love* with the object-relatedness of *loving*. De Rougemont believes, wrongly, that loving the other from "the standpoint of the self" is also the essence of the state of nostalgia, which he views as incompatible with true dialogue between two people who perceive each other distinctly as separate individuals. It should be clear that nostalgia and dialogue should not be mutually exclusive any more than being-in-love should rule out loving. Therefore, de Rougemont's position that the usual fate of the twin narcissism of being-in-love is the destruction of the love relationship and of life itself is highly questionable. He implies that Wagner's Liebestod motif depicts the twin nostalgia for oneness and that the leitmotif music conveys the ecstatic release of dying together: The love of Tristan and Isolde was the anguish of being two (1956, 53). He alludes to altered ego states that also characterize the height of sexual passion, so it is with a note of wry commentary that one looks upon Gottfried's version, the one on which Wagner's opera is based, which has the lovers chaste. Clearly Wagner's music, according to all who have ever listened to it, enrapt, disregarded those aspects of the libretto deriving from Gottfried's puristic notion of asexual nostalgia.

De Rougemont implies that the anguish of the Liebestod experience is related directly to twin narcissism. He describes that anguish as foundering in a twin downrush, being cast into a headlong swoon, an initiation into the dark world of ecstatic release and of death, phenomena which we, as analysts, would regard now as sensations not only of psychic pain but orgastic pleasure, deriving from *early ego states*. These states may be experienced as "good" or "bad," depending on the extent to which conflict about them is resolved and particularly on whether the temporary suspension of certain ego functions in the altered ego state of being-in-love is feared or craved.

Oedipal Longings in the Liebestod

Among the fantasies embedded in the Tristan legend are those deriving from the drinking of the fatal love potion that permits "passion and joy most sharp, and Anguish without end, and Death" (see figure 3). The crucial enactment of drinking the same love potion embodies, reflects, and organizes many themes. Instead of condemning the lovers for their guilt and transgressions, the troubadours' audience, or the masses, admired them, for the love potion provides an alibi that permits their claim to innocence in the eyes of God and frees their passion, which is superimposed by fate, from any connection with human responsibility. The issue of Tristan's guilt or innocence in the eyes of God, an issue that pervades the troubadours' questioning within the legend, hinges on the drinking of the philtre and on the rules of chivalry, in which the fair conqueror always wins. The lovers are not the authors of their actions, so they cannot help gratifying their passionate yearnings that the potion's magic imposed. The potion, originally provided by Iseult's mother, who intended it for her daughter and King Mark, also appears to dissolve Iseult's former hatred of Tristan, whom she had nurtured only when his true identity was unknown to her. So Iseult's hatred is transformed into love. It would seem reasonable to suggest that they are both quite repelled by each other, as they were in fact before they drank of the magic,

HOW SIR TRISTRAM
DRANK OF THE
LOVE DRINK

Figure 3. The drinking of the love potion permits "passion and joy most sharp, and Anguish without end, and Death." (Aubrey Beardsley, book illustration to *La Morte d'Arthur: How Sir Tristram Drank of the Love Drink* [1893]. Victoria and Albert Museum/Art Resource, New York.)

together. Tristan, who loves Mark above all, is forced, despite his will, to love Iseult. Iseult, who hates Tristan because he slew her uncle, is forced to love him now. The legend thus reflects bisexual currents in Tristan's personality and the strong negative oedipal coexisting with the positive oedipal longings. His presumed homosexual motivation is also used to declare innocence—it was all for the love of Mark that the lovers are smitten, for Tristan sacrificed his life to bring Iseult to Mark to gain more of Mark's love and admiration.

There are numerous other indications in the legend that Tristan's primary tie is to King Mark and not to Iseult. Denis de Rougemont's (1956) thorough literary analysis of the legend informs us that an Arthurian knight, like a troubadour, regarded himself as the vassal of some chosen lady when he actually was the vassal of a lord. Tristan's quest for Iseult, before the influence of the love potion, is clearly undertaken to please Mark, with whom his loyalty lies. His heroic feats are designed to seduce her falsely, to present her to the King. The felon barons, who constantly erect obstacles to thwart Tristan's passion, are not so much jealous of his love for Iseult, but are envious of Tristan because he is Mark's favorite. Because of his love for Tristan, Mark does not desire a wife and heir, but agrees to wed only to pacify the felon barons, never intending it seriously. Even after his marriage, Mark has Tristan sleeping in his chambers where he has free access to the queen, and would apparently never have entertained any objection to this arrangement if not for the pressures exerted on him by the envious felon barons.

Other evidence for Tristan's strong loyalty to Mark is to be found in the text describing the lovers' banishment to the woods. Here, Tristan prays to God to give him strength to give Iseult back to Mark, so that he may serve his beloved King again. Iseult also wishes to return to her husband, but primarily to restore Tristan's status with Mark. They have a writ prepared, declaring their innocence. The King considers the writ with the felon barons, and pardons Tristan, concluding that because Tristan wants to prove his right in arms he never loved Iseult with a love dishonorable to the King.

The manifest content here serves, among other functions, to mask guilt over oedipal victory and incestuous consummation. The oedipal themes in this story are atypical with respect to outcome. Tristan, because he never participated in the oedipal triangle, was exempt from the usual oedipal and incestuous prohibitions of childhood. It is not surprising, then, that to be an "oedipal winner," as it were, is part of his fate. This victory is recognizable as a continuation of the theme of Tristan's narcissistic entitlement—a wishful, grandiose fantasy that transgression for him, the favored son, will be understood rather than punished. Indeed, the lovers' banishment to the forest is ended by Mark's erroneous belief, based on the sword's position between them, that they are innocent. They are thus not only exceptions to the laws banning incest but may proceed with the blessings of the wronged father—a classical fantasy of narcissistic entitlement.

The narcissistic entitlement of an oedipal winner has been referred to earlier in this chapter, with regard to Tristan. I shall develop this theme further in the context of the opera *Siegfried*. The God Wotan, disguised as the Wanderer, cedes his oedipal rights of power and supremacy to Siegfried, just as King Mark did to Tristan, when he discovers he can no longer break the spear, Notung, when it is in Siegfried's possession, as he did when it was in the possession of Siegfried's father, Siegmund, and when he recognizes Siegfried's inevitable connection with Brünnhilde. The Wanderer abdicates as he initiates a self-parricidal offering:

> He who can wake her
> he who can win her
> makes me powerless forever. (John 1984, 115)

As noted earlier, fearlessness turns to anguish for Siegfried, upon his falling in love with Brünnhilde. The anguish of the Liebestod appears to allow for the emergence of oedipal guilt even in a man who did not have to master the conflicts of oedipal triangulation, raised as he was only by men for whom he felt contempt and with whom he could not identify, let alone idealize. The existential aspects of the newly developed angst is also related to the fears that with intense love comes the fear of losing what one loves the most. One is reminded of Freud's 1916 essay, "On Transience," in which he deals with the vulnerability of certain individuals who would chose to avoid love, beauty, or other states, ideals, and individuals about whom one might feel passionate attachments. The reason, according to Freud, that these people, whom he regarded as pathologically depressed, avoided those aspects of life which were most appealing and attractive is that the attachments, investments, or cathexes with what must inevitably be transient, leave one vulnerable to the pains and desolation of loss. In the case of Siegfried, the same theme interweaves with the inevitable sequelae of being human, as the Gods gradually give over their power to the human race, as Wotan, or Wanderer, did to Siegfried, the price of this power being the oedipal and existential anxieties under consideration here. Siegfried's new awareness of the heartbeats of love reverberating indistinguishably with the heartbeats of fear in connection with oedipal love is expressed poignantly as he becomes aware of the first stirrings of love upon his first contact with the sleeping Brünnhilde, thinking, as we noted earlier, that this first encounter with any woman is in fact with his dead mother, Sieglinde:

> Anguish and yearning
> conquer my courage;
> on my heart beating wildly
> trembles my hand.
> Am I a coward?
> Is this what fear is?
> Oh mother! Mother!
> Your bold fearless child
> A woman lies here in sleep
> and she now has taught me to fear!
> Then life I shall gather
> from lips filled with sweetness
> what though I die by this kiss. (John 1984, 118)

Brünnhilde, awakening, voices the words that clearly indicate the feelings of the merger of Liebestod, as each remains lost in radiant, rapt contemplation of the other:

> Your eyes alone could behold me;
> my heart to you alone wakes.

In his confusion of sleep, death, and merger during this love duet, Siegfried cries,

> My mother is alive, then?
> Sleep enfolded her here?

As Brünnhilde corrects him in her explanation to him of Liebestod oneness:

> Nevermore you'll look on your mother,
> but we are one. (119)

Dying is thus juxtaposed inevitably with living in Siegfried's prophetic anticipation of the Liebestod, for humans are not immortal, as are the gods.

It is important at this point to note that one of the five versions of the legend, Gottfried's, on which Wagner's opera, *Tristan und Isolde* is based, has the lovers chaste: their union is never consummated. This version, unlike the others, does not mask the critical superego and oedipal prohibitions, for it appears to express certain oedipal features of traditional courtly love whereby the idealized but unattainable lady is admired and adored only from a distance. Because she represents an incestuous object, Tristan's adoration is compromised by his regarding sexual contact with her as low and debased, not compatible with tenderness. In all other versions of the Tristan legend, Tristan starts with a sin against courtly love, traditionally chaste, by actual physical possession of a real woman. This sinfulness, representing oedipal and incestuous enactment, is painfully redeemed, despite Mark's forgiveness, by the penance the lovers undergo.

The belief and proclamation of the populace that the lovers are innocent of incest, even when guilt is too visible to be denied, may be understood as an instance of mass denial, and would appear to be related to primal-scene disavowal and the wish to live the lives of Tristan and Iseult vicariously. That the King and the people are fooled by the sword between them is, on their part, sheer falsification of the facts, like the child's insistence of the parents' chastity, but the falsification is welcomed by all as an opportunity to deny the feelings of painful exclusion inherent in witnessing the primal scene. So long as Tristan and Iseult can prove their innocence by ordeals and the painful overcoming of obstacles, arbitrary as those may seem, they are happily exonerated by all. Obstacles in the legend serve important functions not just as literary devices around which the plot turns, but, in parallel fashion, also serve psychological needs of the protagonists. The next section of this chapter will deal with the functions of obstacles to the fulfillment of passionate yearnings.

Romantic Love and the Liebestod: Sadomasochism or Conflict over Merger and Autonomy

The romantic love songs of the troubadours are nearly all characterized by (1) an idealization of the state of being-in-love, (2) putting obstacles in the way of fulfillment of passionate longings, and (3) the death from grief of one lover upon the death of the other. A study of some of the manifest contradictions in the myth will be used to shed some light on the intrapsychic function of obstacles to the fulfillment of love, and how it relates to the love-death.

The Function of Obstacles in the Legend

Before romantic love became part of the enlarged vocabulary of the Middle Ages, according to Bergmann (1987), it was taken for granted that the expected path of lovers' journeys ends in their coming together, that is, in their orgastic sexual union. In this new species of love, unconsummated love was idealized, and the usual climactic finale was postponed, almost indefinitely. To effect this prolongation of a state of desire, the man endured hardships for the sake of his lady, and both lovers would devise extreme plans involving putting obstacles in the way of normal sexual union. These maneuvers guaranteed that the love would remain unrequited and/or unconsummated as long as possible.

De Rougemont presents some interesting ideas about the omnipresence in the plots of the romantic novels of obstacles that apparently contradict the manifestly expressed wishes of the lovers to consummate their love. He feels that the manifest contradictions of lovers placing obstacles in the path of the fulfillment of that very love which craves fulfillment reflect the author's intention to describe the lovers' secret quest for the "obstructions that foster love." Passion, he said, with the theological bias of his time and place, is inevitably linked with self-destruction for anyone yielding uncompromisingly to it; it leads ultimately to death, and that is the primary disguised content of the myth. Although there is room to question that author's gloomy predictions about the inevitable fatal outcome of passion, he is correct in saying that it is precisely the manifestly arbitrary character of the obstructions introduced into the tale that may reveal its latent content and elucidate some aspects of the passion with which it is concerned. After all, Tristan, the slayer of giants and dragons, is a man of unusual prowess and cunning and therefore in an unquestionably favorable position to carry on his affair with Iseult unimpeded. His ambivalence about doing so, and hers as well, is never questioned in the legend, so that their behavior in not choosing the path of least resistance is indeed a contradiction in the plot. De Rougemont says that objectively not one of the barriers to the fulfillment of their love is insuperable, yet each time they give up, never missing a chance to be separated. When there is no obstruction, they invent one in order to intensify their passion, which requires coercively imposed obstacles in order to be perpetuated. His major thesis is that the legend is primarily about partings in the name of passion in order that the lovers may intensify their love even at the cost of their happiness and their lives. This typical Liebestod subtheme appears also in *Siegfried,* as in the hero's wish, "through fire I shall make her mine." The ordeal by fire, the major ordeal in this opera, is found in many romantic legends, as an obstacle which brands and fosters passion.

Updike once again (1994) captures the function of obstacles in *Brazil,* his modern fictional parable of the Tristan legend. His protagonists, Tristão and Isabel, are beset by poverty, familial objections, violence, and reversals of fortune along every step of the way in realizing their passionate, fateful liaison. In an interesting twist, Updike does not allow Isabel's fateful attraction to culminate in fatal reunion with her lover. She must get on with her more pedestrian life as her wish to lie down on the beach and die with her murdered Tristão is thwarted. The final obstacle to eternal reunion, to translating the wish into the will to die together, is provided by some inner life force mirrored by the jarring voice of her uncle "crying out, 'for God's sake, Isabel!' in sheer embarrassment at this vulgar display of Brazilian romanticism" (260).

De Rougemont was correct in saying that the function of struggles and obstacles is to maintain the intensity of passion. However, he was talking only of drastic kinds of obstacles that ultimately destroy love, and failed to underscore the importance, in the real lives of living lovers, of those more "normal" obstacles that can also preserve love, enhancing regard and loving concern for the object, keeping the love alive, and not culminating in a literal love-death. Person (1989), in her sympathetic view of the positive values of romantic love, believes that courtships always involve a series of tests of love, tests in which one lover repeatedly asks the other to prove sincerity. This normal courtship ritual can, of course, escalate into a full inhibition of loving, especially when the fear of rejection once one has committed oneself to loving is so strong. At its most pathological extreme, this normal courtship ritual of renewed expressions of doubts of love embodies the wish, belief, illusion, or delusion that a guarantee of no rejection can occur only after the obstacle course eventuates in the death of one or both lovers: "I love you so much I'd die for you, I'd die without you, and I shall prove it." The question to be raised now is this: Is the promise of realization mainly a threat with unquestionable sadomasochistic overtones, or does it also suggest that more subtle motivations can be found in the perpetuation of the pain and agony of humiliation?

Sadomasochism

The classical explanation of obstacles, suffering, and maintaining the intensity of passion is that the romantic love of the troubadours and of the nineteenth-century romantics is essentially sadomasochistic. In these art forms, we note the important characterization of the teasingly unavailable seductress, the "femme fatale." The idolization of the femme fatale in the troubadours' rendering of romanticism has been considered as epitomizing a sadomasochistic form of love. Sadomasochism is reflected in the troubadour ballad hallmark of the abject lover worshipping from a distance the cold, disdainful, aloof woman, seizing every opportunity to hone passion by placing obstacles in the way of fulfillment and cultivating suffering. That suffering is inflicted upon the self and upon both lovers.

The phenomenon of lovers' self-creation of obstacles when none are in fact imposed from without is what has been called the masochism of romanticism. The theme of all the romantic plots is that passion means suffering. Evans (1953) tells us that the main characteristic of troubadour love is that the lady is worshipped from a *distance*. She is cold, disdainful, aloof, while the lover is abject. The strength of his love is demonstrated by his capacity to suffer. Evans sees the haughty, aloof mistress, the abject lover, and the technique of avoidance as the basic ingredients of the troubadour concept of love, and this, he says, is the masochistic prototype. The woman who is idolized is the femme fatale who, he feels, represents the preoedipal mother.

In his *Vita Nuova*, Dante (1294) develops an Italian Renaissance version of the medieval troubadours' hallmark sadomasochism. The poet is smitten and undone by his love for the gracious and glorious, yet distant and then dead Beatrice (see figure 2). He is self-obsessed and self-pitying in his subjugation to Love, a personified male figure, seen also in Burne-Jones's painting, *Chant d'Amour* (see book jacket illustration). Love controls the smitten, who must tend to his every pleasure, but Dante's mission is to transcend this sadomasochism by examining his new life in a dedication to the search for meaning. The romantic love themes of the troubadours convey the man's desperate attempt to repudiate his succumbing again to the originally passive role which, as a boy, he had managed to escape. When a man does not surrender himself in emotional attachments, according to Evans, it is because this involves succumbing to his deep masochism of the preoedipal period. Ergo, when he does surrender, he is masochistic.

If the femme fatale derives from the preoedipal mother imago, and if that imago is nonspecific as to gender (Pollock 1975; Bergmann 1980), there could also be a male equivalent of the femme fatale in adult relationships to whom the woman either submits or fears to submit masochistically. Clinically, this seems to be the case. Such a pattern is also typical of many homosexual love affairs.

In the legend of Tristan and Iseult, masochism is clearly presumed in the following summary of self-imposed obstacles I have prepared:

> The lovers have been apart for two years and Tristan, not hearing from Iseult, assumes she does not love him. In his misery, he marries another woman, also named Iseult, whom he does not love. Finally, he receives a report that with all the time and distance between them, Iseult his love, is pining away. Somehow Iseult learns that Tristan did not face a foe conjured in her name. She feels this is a betrayal, so when Tristan finally finds a way to meet her, she sends a message that she will not see him. Tristan sends a messenger back to tell Iseult that he really loves her, but she does not believe what she hears. Tristan, disguising himself as a leper, tries to see her, but she spurns him— although in private, she pines away. Downcast, Tristan sails away. Iseult repents, realizing she has been unjust. To punish herself, she puts on a hairshirt. Tristan, now home again, languishes because Iseult has driven him away. He wants to die, but also wants Iseult to know that it is for love of her. He returns to her, disguised as a beggar. As a ruse, he simulates madness, shaves his head, dyes his skin, and gets into court. In this condition, he says his name is Tristan and that he loves Iseult. He asks Mark to give her to him. At first Iseult refuses to believe he is Tristan, but when he proves his identity, they resume their love trysts once more. But a felon baron is onto them. Tristan flees, but only after he and she agree that he will summon her to die with him when his death becomes inevitable.

This summary illustrates the legend's central emphasis on repeated self-creation of obstacles, culminating in a Liebestod, which Evans and others view as essentially masochistic. The greater the belief of one that the love is unrequited, or that the lover is indifferent, the greater the yearning for the apparently withholding one. The lovers take turns acting and feeling first in control and then victimized, all on the basis of their illusions. This is the prototype of masochism in romantic literature.

So we see throughout the story numerous "degradation trips." Does this two-year development of the lovers' mutual distrust reflect, as Evans and others contend, only the pathological form of love, sadomasochism, or does it contain other important implications? It is my belief that suffering and pain as part of the human condition, as an existential given, and the need for punishment of oedipally related transgressions do not always or exclusively imply sadomasochism. Rejection, scorn, suffering, and the wish to die are pathological variations of the conditions normally required for arousal in all love relationships, those found in life as well as in art.

Freud (1912) said that obstacles are normally required to heighten libido and "where natural resistances to satisfaction have not been sufficient men have at all times erected conventional ones so as to be able to enjoy love" (187). Rejection, scorn, the deliberate placement of obstacles to romantic and sexual fulfillment, and a flirting with death, are well-understood as pathological variations of the raising of normal arousal thresholds, which we see in milder versions in normal love relationships. Pathology enters an otherwise normal picture when attempts to increase the intensity of passion escalate to sadomasochistic extremes. This normal increase in intensity stands in contrast to the torments depicted by the troubadours. An optimal degree of self-imposition of obstacles is, as Freud implied, a normal technique of lovemaking, enhancing the entire experience and facilitating maximal pleasurable orgastic discharge. However, when there are significant sadomasochistic predispositions in the partners, a seeming readiness for this normal technique emerges manifestly as the sadomasochism depicted so persuasively in the romantic novels. That very sadomasochism may sometimes serve a restitutive function for vulnerable individuals, helping to restore self-object differentiation when boundaries between self and other have suffered even transiently in a state of being-in-love or during passionate sexual arousal. The lovers' self-imposed obstacles may also function as devices aimed at ensuring an unambivalent state of union. Heightening of passionate intensity, by creating external obstacles, permits a "split" whereby love is preserved in a passionate unity and hatred directed toward the obstacle-ridden outer world.

The important relation between love and hate in the being-in-love state is discussed by Bergmann (1971) who says that in order to be able to love, early object representations must be benign and cathected more with libido than with aggression. Considerations of masochism, however, must enter any discussion of painful states of longing (see Bergmann 1980). On the other hand, the state of longing and yearning need not be painful per se, but only under certain conditions when it is self-perpetuated, as in a prolonged state of unrequited love; when the feelings of yearning and longing are cathected more than the object is; and when it precludes, because of its intensity, any integrative efforts of the ego to respond to the reality of the other person and thereby maintain object constancy. Since the oedipal issues in romantic love have received reasonably extensive coverage in the classical psychoanalytic literature, I have chosen to give priority, in my discussion, to certain relatively neglected preoedipal features.

Distance Regulation, Autonomy, and Merger: The Rapprochement Crisis

Does the lovers' cultivation of suffering in the Tristan legend symbolize only the pathological form of love, sadomasochism, or does it reflect other developmental vicissitudes? Sometimes it is hard to make a differential diagnosis. Romantic love, carried to pathological extremes, frequently crosses the line to perverse forms, including corruption, enslavement, masochistic surrender, and other forms of sadomasochism or subversion of the self. This is particularly so, according to Person (1989) when a strong core of identity and self-worth are lacking. When the impulse to submerge one's self is so strong, and autonomy is sacrificed to the point of literal or symbolic suicide, the playful, pleasurable aspects of ecstasy become perverted into serious pathology, as in the example of *The Blue Angel,* in which an enthralled professor is seduced into extreme humiliation and ultimately death by the dark lady Lola's erotic powers. Other pathological variants of romantic love are seen in certain characteristically disturbed deviations in normal ego development, including altered, pathological ego states or states of consciousness. When the lover appears more in love with death than with the pleasures of merger, we are on firm ground in making our distinctions. Other times, it is not so easy. Not every wish to merge carries with it the lethal finality of degrading submission to the femme fatale, who is the seductress symbolizing death, or her male equivalent with similar erotic power. The prototype of that image is to be found in the Burne-Jones painting, *The Depths of the Sea* (see figure 4).

The sadomasochism in the Tristan and Iseult mode of loving also reflects an attempt at distance regulation (Gediman 1981), and may be conceptualized, even reformulated, in terms of a particular resolution of the rapprochement crisis (Mahler 1972; Mahler, Pine, and Bergman 1975) which embodies the typical conflicts of the preoedipal phase. Intensifying passion by obstacles to its fulfillment may be viewed as a way of mastering the anxiety of achieving individuation and separateness, a sign of adaptive ego functioning, when they conflict with the desire for fusion in a symbiotic unity or a sense of oneness (Kaplan 1978). The swooning and revival waves of Wagner's Liebestod leitmotif evoke memories and reminiscences of lifelong rhythmic patterns, of feeling states connected with arousal and relaxation, of approaching and distancing, merging and separation, as they are echoed in the later developed patterns of passionate sexual arousal and orgasm. That is, the musical leitmotif captures what is also depicted in the written legend: the comings and goings of the rapprochement crisis.

The rhythms of parting and coming together, the theme of all courtly love myths, might be viewed as derivatives of the rapprochement rhythms of establishing optimal distance between two people, both literally and intrapsychically (see Bouvet 1958), with normal and pathological variants. The regulation of passionate intensity, then, is not exclusively sadomasochistic, although the work of the ego in functioning adaptively may be fueled by the same sexual and aggressive drives that characterize the more pathological sadomasochistic resolution. Nor does it necessarily exclude a loving concern

Figure 4. The lethal finality of submission to the "femme fatale" or her male equivalent with similar erotic power. Sir Edward Burne-Jones, *The Depths of the Sea* [1887]. Courtesy of the Fogg Art Museum, Harvard University Art Museums.)

for the object. We can indeed open a normative window on the pathological. The "exquisite anguish" in the yielding swoon of the lovers casts its spell because it is evocative not only of sexual passion but also of the early ego state of fusion and merging. The swoon without the effort of the mind—the ego's functioning work to achieve individuation and separateness—could be understood as psychological death, as opposed to psychological birth, or living.

A poetic rendition of the preoedipal distance-regulation conflict, or that between merger and autonomy, oneness and separateness, is to be found in the Liebestod love duet between Siegfried and Brünnhilde in last act of the opera *Siegfried*. Siegfried, in profound agitation while throwing Brünnhilde looks of passionate yearning, begins by expressing his anxieties about his former sense of omnipotence giving way to his present vulnerability to fear of death as he desires to merge with his beloved:

> In bonds of fear
> I have been bound
>   from you alone
>   could I learn how to fear
>   Since you have bound me
>   in powerful fetters
> give me my freedom again.
>   . . . .
>
>   Now a glorious maid
>   has wounded my heart;
>   wounds in my head
>   were struck by that maid
> I came with no shield or helm. (John 1984, 120).

Brünnhilde, for her part, echoes similar sentiments, hoping to avert the catastrophe she fears will ensue from an excess of passion:

>   Do not come near me
>   with passionate frenzy
>   do not pursue me
>   with masterful might
> Or else you'll destroy all our love.
>   . . . .

> Love yourself
> and leave me in peace;
> destroy not this maid who is yours! (122–23)

Siegfried responds to Brünnhilde's prophetic annunciation of death in this Liebestod motif, hoping that the deadly aspects of passionate merger can be avoided if only their feelings for each other are of an equal intensity:

> I love you
> did you but love me. (123)

The couple finally seem to set each other at ease about the fusion and merger of their identities as their passion continues into the last opera of the Ring Cycle, *Götterdämmerung:*

> BRÜNNHILDE: Then you are Siegfried and Brünnhilde!
> SIEGFRIED: Where I am both are united . . .
> BRÜNNHILDE: Apart, who can divide us?
> Divided, still we are one. (John 1985, 71)

To round up our considerations of the easy confusion, or conflations of meaning of sadomasochism and distance regulation, it is fitting here to turn to the ideas of Hermann (1936), who speaks of clinging and going-in-search, a pair of contrasting instincts which are precursors of sadism and masochism—of roaming and wandering as derivatives of yearning to reestablish the original union with the mother. The sadism and masochism, as well as the propensity toward suffering for other reasons, that are represented in Tristan and Iseult's many partings and returnings, could also be viewed usefully as derivative of these early trends, as Hermann feels many such intense relationships are. Tristan's urge to roam, especially, is not simply counterphobic, simply a form of "heroic masochism." We may also see in the Houdiniesque elements of adventure and escape, the tidal-wave feel of coming perilously close to danger followed by heroic escapes and then aimless wandering attempts to escape from the dreaded primary maternal engulfment that threatens each time the yearning for blissful reunion is enacted. Tristan's adventures suggest a fusion fantasy, fantasies of death and denial of death through rebirth and the fantasies of a "great escape artist." The theme of repeated partings, wandering far and then returning, also suggest the wish-fear of the claustrum, or the conflicts specific to the oral triad (Lewin 1946). The "masochism," the suffering attendant on the placement of obstacles in the way of fulfillment of passion, serves the lovers in their attempts to regulate distance, to find the optimal balance of "oneness and separateness" in boundary formation, and in that sense reflects an adaptive level of ego functioning.

The lovers repeat these echoes of preoedipal trauma and conflict in endless variations, which they then attempt to master by alternating rhythmically their self-created obstacles and distrust with their blissful reunions. From this point of view, the comings and goings of Tristan and Iseult and the obstacles they place between themselves express both the wish and the fear of symbiotic fusion and merger. The wish may reflect a defensive regression prompted by oedipal anxieties or a repetition of the bliss of original symbiosis; the fear may reflect the drive to advance to new libidinal positions and the thrust of the drive for ego autonomy and growth that preserve the sense of self and separateness.

Suicide and the Liebestod

According to Flügel (1953), Liebestod fantasies, of love, death, and dying together, express a wish not for a cessation of life, but for "intrauterine omnipotence," for Nirvana, a life of peace after death, or what I have called the "good" death. There is very little in the psychoanalytic literature about dying together. Freud (1913) states that if a man is faced with the necessity of death, he tends to deny it with a woman's love, suggesting a related Liebestod motif, if not precisely the dying-together phenomenon. Later (1917), however, he states, "In the two most opposed situations of being most intensely in love and of suicide the ego is overwhelmed by the object, though in totally different ways" (67). Suicides in the state of melancholia that represent a dying together may also reflect this pathological introjection into the ego of the ambivalently loved lost object, where the lost loved-and-hated one lives on as a part of the self.

It was Ernest Jones who wrote specifically on dying together in two separate papers. The first (1911) makes reference to Heinrich von Kleist's suicide—also mentioned recently by Binion (1993), who concluded that Kleist, turned on by dying women, found one to join him in suicide—and concludes that most psychoanalysts would probably agree that the wish to die together is the same as the wish to sleep and lie together, originally, of course, with the mother. He also reminds us of the primal connection between ideas of travel and death that relate to fantasies of dying together. The second Jones paper (1912) concerns an actual event of a man and a wife who perished together at Niagara Falls in a dangerous situation which nonetheless could have been escaped were it not for the woman crying, "I can't go on. Let us die here!" whereupon neither made an effort at self-preservation or to rescue the other. Jones explains the double suicide as representing birth, where the childless couple, making use of the unconscious connection between the womb and the grave, equate their wish to have a child with death: it is a suicide with no suicidal intent, but where the wish to die in the arms of the beloved represents a wish to beget a child with the loved one, and at another level, a return to the mother's womb.

Zilboorg (1938) said that in

> murder-suicide pacts, the drive toward death, always with the flag of immortality in hand, carried with it the fantasy of joining the dead or dying, or being joined in death. The latter is particularly prominent among the double suicides of lovers. There is hardly a primitive race which does not have a lovers' volcano (Japan), a lovers' waterfall (Bali) or a lovers' rock from which the lovers jump so that they may be joined in the beyond. (179)

Pollock's (1976) paper, "Manifestations of Abnormal Mourning: Homicide and Suicide Following the Death of Another," surveys documented double suicides throughout the world's history and cultures, concluding that each bears the hallmark of a significant reaction from the past, reflecting uncompleted and pathological mourning. Pollock believes that what may look like identification in the suicide may be more reflective of the wish to reunite with the one from whom the separation occurred. He invokes Kohut's (1971) concepts of the merger, the mirror, and the twinship to account for the phenomenon. Suicides attempting reunion in a life after death are explicitly linked by Brodsky (1957) to Liebestod fantasies. In describing a case of a woman's wish to die after the death of her brother, he says:

> In some of the material from this case, it seemed clear that the brother was really a substitute for the unsatisfying mother. The fantasy of being eternally asleep in the grave with a surrogate of the maternal object suggests that Lewin's oral triad of wishes is at the basis of *Liebestod* fantasies. . . . Lewin has in this connection equated good death with good sleep. (15)

Binion (1993), in his study of the love-death connection in art and literature, catalogues double suicide love-deaths, citing, among other works, Heine's 1830 *Die Flucht,* in which one couple drowns together, and his 1856 *Jammertal,* which envisions a pair of lovers "hissing and crying, laughing and sighing as they froze to death" (Binion 1993, 17). Binion also refers to lovers hugging awkwardly in midair as they plunged to their death and to Max Klinger's "lovers locked in postmortem improprieties amidst a sea of darkness" (17; see figure 5 in this volume).

While the next chapter deals with a contrast between normal and pathological outcomes of Liebestod fantasies, this chapter concludes with a few other examples of the "good death" as understood, along with the above cross-cultural examples of joint suicides, as normative cultural contexts to accommodate what from an individual psychological point of view may yet bear many stigmata of the pathological. Returning once again to the work of Person (1989), who has studied cultural aspects of romantic love, we learn that

> in Japan, where conformity and identification with the group are valued above all, romantic love does not have a high priority. However, the Japanese do celebrate one highly romantic convention [referred to above]: lovers who cannot be together in life join each other in death—by suicide. For the Japanese, self-will (and its potential for disharmony with the mores and dictates of the group) cannot exist within the cultural framework. Consequently, the only acceptable out-

Figure 5. "Lovers locked in postmortem improprieties amidst a sea of darkness." (Max Klinger after Edvard Munch, "Finis," from a series of etchings, *Ein Leben* [1881]. Kunsthalle, Bremen. Foto Marburg/Art Resource, New York.)

let for love (which is dependent on self will) is doomed love, in which the lovers, by dying for their love, simultaneously assert and extinguish the self, thus insuring that the group is undamaged by the individualism of the lover. Stories of doomed love are sanctioned by the Japanese as a means of channeling illicit desires in a way consonant with the cultural demand for conformity and duty. The Japanese weep at stories of doomed lovers' suicides, and thereby vicariously indulge, romanticize, and exorcise those impulses within themselves. This kind of dynamic sheds little light on why doomed love has been celebrated at moments in the West during those periods of time when the valuation of autonomy was coming into its ascendancy, but the individual's behavior was still bound by strict laws of fealty and obligation, for example in the Middle Ages. In such times the outcome of pre-emptory love must of necessity be the Liebestod. (132)

These mass, cultural investments in the Liebestod would appear, then, to serve as a safeguard against the hazards of too much autonomy, for romantic love always channels the potentiality for acting on "illicit" desires and narcissistic disregard for the natural (in this case socio-cultural) order of things. This would seem to be the case for both the East and the West. The paradox is to indulge narcissistic impulses pathologically, but safely, when they challenge the stable order of things. De Rougemont attempted with great difficulty to grapple with this paradox in romantic love in the Western World. He missed the essence of the delicate balance between the pathological and the normative in the Liebestod. The missing link can be found in the idea of simultaneously asserting and extinguishing the self, suggesting a compromise formation between wishes for the "good death" via merging the self with another and wishes to ward off the "bad death" via self-perpetuation. When the conflict is resolved, we see more normality than the pathology of an unresolved imbalance of forces of ego advancement and ego dissolution. The normal and the pathological are subject to the rules of compromise and conflict resolution.

Three

The Normal and the Pathological in the Liebestod

*T*here are many ways in which painful states of longing and yearning blend from the normal into the pathological, as when they are self-perpetuated in an unbridled manner in cases of unrequited love and when the integrative efforts of the ego to respond to the reality of the other person are weak. Person (1989) takes the position that in fact passionate attachments belong in the realm of normal psychology, though a certain minority are permeated with derivatives of intrapsychic conflict. She maintains that it does not follow that love is not worth the pain any more than one would suggest that life's existential limitations make life not worth living. However, she rightly notes, as I shall illustrate, that love can unleash destructive forces as it becomes perverse, devouring, and self-abnegating.

I have already contrasted the pathology of sadomasochism with the normality of "merger" and individuation as developmental phases. However, here is the paradox: as Person has already noted, the impulse to merge is potentially at odds with another aim of love. One seeks to lose the self in merger, but one must lose it with an Other. In total merger from an intrapsychic point of view, there would be no other, except in the eyes of the other and of any empathic outside observers of the merger. Thus, says Person, the concrete fulfillment of fantasies of merger carries with it the threat of the symbolic annihilation of the self and of the other. Love, by its nature, committed to the preservation of the beloved as well as the self, cannot press through to its goal. The political theorist Hans Morgenthau (1962) presents the dilemma: the reunion in love can never be complete for any length of time except in the Liebestod, which destroys the lovers by uniting them. Liebestod, in its normative sense, however, must be understood both as a fantasy and a realization in the context of oscillation—which permits complete merger through the reunion of two individuals while leaving their own individualities intact. The dilemma is thus resolved on the side of the normative. It is the failure of this resolution that will constitute the bulk of my examples of the pathological. Both lovers want separateness, both want oneness, and both are developmentally programmed (Mahler 1972; Mahler, Pine, and Bergman 1975; Kaplan 1978) to resolve this dilemma of the rapprochement period and to avoid the otherwise annihilatory ending of the Liebestod. They want to be one but they also want to preserve each other's individuality for the sake of that love for each other. Ideas about death in the Liebestod do not, to my mind, exclude this resolution.

While this attempt to resolve the paradox gets to the normative aspects of the Liebestod, the desire to dominate, to insure possession, to merge, can result in the most extreme pathological outcomes. When the lover kills himself and his beloved, there is a literal enactment of the perversion of the Liebestod. This chapter will outline the factors distinguishing one outcome from the other.

Some Pathological Variations

Turning once again to the torments sung by the troubadours, one sees how benign they are compared with those detailed by the nineteenth-century romanticists. Mario Praz, in *The Romantic Agony* (1951), presents an analysis of themes in nineteenth-century romantic literature, including Frankensteinian vampirism and de Sade's deadly sex, among others. More recently, Binion (1993) elaborated on the fantasy of loving to death, giving as one example Kleist's 1808 stage shocker *Penthesilea,* in which "the Amazon queen and Achilles tore at each other's flesh until she kissed him to death" (Binion 1993, 15). Most representative would be the guilty lovers in Adolf Müllner's 1813 drama of guilty lovers, *Die Schuld,* in which "he stripped her of her flesh like a lusty beast of prey while she stabbed him and sucked out his blood in her embrace" (Binion 1993, 15). De Rougemont considered this literary genre a degradation of the myth of the romantic troubadours of medieval times, of which the Tristan myth is prototypical. In the latter-day works, the agony of suicide was replaced by that of sexual perversions and fatal sex. In the Tristan legend, too, the theme of fatal sex underlies the love-death, and de Rougemont tells us that it is only through death that relief from the pain of complete union of passion can be achieved.

Perversion, Murder, and Suicide

However, the fatal sex that is a degradation of the Tristan myth is quite different from the fatal sex in that Celtic myth. Richard Strauss's opera *Salomé* (Polachek 1964) based on Oscar Wilde's play, illustrates the perverse, devouring, and self-abnegating extremes to which these nineteenth-century derivations of the Liebestod fantasy may go. While this story reflects a Liebestod theme, one which Binion designates along with that of Judith and Holofernes as a one-sided love-death in art, it is a prototypically pathological one, but it well illustrates how Liebestod fantasies can be ordered on a spectrum ranging from the normal to the most pathological. When the opera was first presented in 1905 in Dresden, the composer's colleagues were horrified by the decadent subject matter of a fourteen-year-old girl's fatal and necrophilic sexual attraction to the decapitated head of Jokanaan, which she receives as a gift for dancing, after stripping seven veils, naked for her stepfather, Herod. People still feel horror, however, because the macabre story is accompanied by sensuous, erotic music, and the intimate connection of the macabre with the erotic seems out of character with love and beauty as we customarily think of them together. The effects on American audiences were so terrible, that the Metropolitan Opera banned its production after its 1907 premiere for twenty-seven years. The overt degeneration of the young girl's character, in juxtaposition with the erotic and the decadent, places this work, insofar as it reflects the girl's fantasy life, squarely in the category of a perversion of the Liebestod.

While the man, Jokanaan, is still alive, he exerts a deathly fascination upon Salomé who, enamored of his deathly pallor, begs him, despite his constant and disgusted refusals, for a kiss, beside herself with the unfulfilled longing that underlies all Liebestod fantasies, the normal as well as the obviously pathological. With the innocent naiveté of a young child, she asks her stepfather Herod, who offers her a reward of anything she wishes if only she would dance for him, for Jokanaan's head on a silver platter so that she can seek revenge on her unrequiting lover while indulging her perverse fantasy in action. There is nothing more evocative than the German language, "Ich will den Kopf des Jochanaan," to express the vulgarity in the self-indulgent girl's demand for the head of the man whose deathly charms have stimulated her obsession for making love to his dismembered body part. Although Herod tries to distract her into accepting as her reward something nice, like jewels, through some ruse of her colluding mother, Herodias, the girl's wish is granted. There is, in fact, some important background reference in the libretto (Polachek 1964) to the coming of the Messiah, the awakening of the dead, and to how terrible it would be to raise them, suggesting a resurrection as well as a Liebestod motif in the composer's thoughts about the sacrilegious symbolism of the spectacle. Portions of the libretto convey the flavor of perverse but ecstatic sexual love inspired by the idea of a vengeful romance powered by literally death-connected matters of the flesh. As Salomé seizes her reward for dancing for her stepfather, she passionately addresses Jokanaan as though he still lived and was participating in a love duet, which is in fact a demented monologue with profuse cannibalistic imagery, delivered exhibitionistically for the onlooking witnesses to hear and see:

> I thirst for your manly beauty; I hunger to touch your flesh. Not wine nor apples can appease my fierce desire. What shall I do now, Joka-

naan? Neither waters nor the raging torrents could ever quench my burning, searing passion. Oh! But why did you look away? Had you but looked on my face you would have loved me too! Yes, I am sure you would have loved me too. *And the great mystery of loving is greater than the mystery of dying.* (13 [emphasis mine])

It is clear that this is her Liebestod fantasy only, for only in her mind does the man participate in this perverse version, as opposed to most other Liebestod scenes in opera in which two lovers share the same fantasy in their interactions in the love-death scenes. The final scene closes with Salomé's orally gratifying kiss on the mouth of the dead man's head, a scene which many audiences cannot bear to look at because of its revolting explicitness, contenting themselves with listening to the beautiful and erotically charged musical accompaniment:

> Ah! Now at last I have kissed your mouth, Jokanaan. Ah! I now at last have kissed your lips. Was it the taste of blood? Nay! But perchance it is thus that love tastes? They say that the taste of love is bitter . . . I pay no heed . . . no heed . . . I have now kissed your mouth, Jokanaan. I have impressed a kiss upon your mouth. (14)

With this final enactment, Herod can bear it no longer and orders Salome killed. Her Liebestod thus ends in death by murder, as she joins her fantasized lover in death, albeit not by conscious choice, as in most Liebestod scenarios. Psychoanalytic speculators, however, would grant themselves the poetic license to interpret that her necrophilic perversion of the Liebestod (see figure 6) indicates that unconsciously she wished to join with him in this way, for motives of degenerate revenge, if not others as well.

Chapter 2 emphasized elements of normal fusion and merger in the Siegfried-Brünnhilde Liebestod of the love duet in the last act of *Siegfried* (John 1984), but here it must be said that there are times, as in the last act of *Götterdämmerung* (John 1985) in which vengeful, murderous wishes distort the love part of the love-death. Brünnhilde in Act II feels betrayed when Siegfried, disguised as Gunther, seizes the ring from her hand. She believes the Gods have wrought this doom and at that point wishes for Siegfried's death simply as a

Figure 6. A nineteenth-century necrophilic perversion of the Liebestod. (Patricia O'Sullivan, *Salomé,* watercolor [1899]. Courtesy, Patricia O'Sullivan and the Metropolitan Opera Guild.)

revenge and not as an opportunity for reunion. Brünnhilde's Liebes-tod thus is motivated by murderous feelings for her erstwhile lover for betraying her and by her anger at the Gods for dooming her love:

> For his treachery he must die
> Strike him and kill him
> For he has betrayed every vow
> and falsehood now he has sworn
> . . . .
> So the death of one
> now must content me
> Siegfried's death
> atones his crime and yours.
> (Porter translation, John 1985, 102, 107)

Chapter 2 reviewed the psychoanalytic literature on double and mass suicides, with particular emphasis on the common equation of the good death with the good sleep of blissful connection. I add now a consideration of the more pathological forms of murder-suicide pacts, such as in the mass suicides of the Reverend Jones's Guyana Temple of Peace, and the Branch Davidians in Waco, Texas. In each of these tragedies, an entire population appeared to suspend the ego function of normal judgment and extinguished itself in the fatal attraction to a charismatic cult leader who offered a utopia of blissful reunion through death. A few additional examples merit mention. One, from literature, concerns the symbolic suicide in the fatal bridge collapse in Thornton Wilder's 1927 novel, *The Bridge of San Luis Rey.* In that work, we find an allegory of mass suicide, in which each individual who perished in the fatal bridge collapse was, in his or her dreams, dying together with a loved one from whom there was in fact no longer any hope of reciprocated love. Wilder sensitively picks up on themes of grief and rage in the unrequited love which, allegori-cally speaking, motivated the mass "suicide," a metaphor for the tragic consequence of the fatal attractions of unrequited love.

Alvarez (1971) reports that in Sylvia Plath's periodic suicide at-tempts, the poet was dealing primarily with her anxieties and guilt about surviving her dead father. Death, for her, was a debt to be met, in the form of suicidal gestures, once every decade. To pay with her life, which she eventually succeeded in doing, also involved the fantasy of joining or regaining her beloved father. It was a passionate act, filled as much with love as with hatred and despair. She had, says Alvarez, a queer conception of the adult as a survivor, "an imaginary Jew from the concentration camp of the mind." In her poem "Daddy" (1961), she includes the lines

> At twenty I tried to die
> And get back to you
> I thought even the bones would do. (51)

What determines the outcome of the Liebestod fantasy? When does the state of being-in-love precipitate death, particularly dual death, and when does it lead to the happy outcome of love and *creative mastery* of fatalism and fatal attractions? Before continuing on with additional examples of the pathological, I should like to return briefly to a general consideration of the normal and the pathological in the Liebestod, with particular emphasis on degrees of ego regression, for this is critical to what distinguishes the normal from the pathological. Some would stress the pathological in the ego regression of any revival of merger states, while others remind us that the integrative capacities of the ego remain intact despite powerfully motivating Liebestod fantasies. Fantasies of rejoining the dead via symbiotic reunion with an omniscient, omnipotent figure can have varying outcomes along a continuum ranging from normality to the pathology of individual, dual, and mass suicide. For example, symbiotic fantasies of dying or killing oneself in order to reunite with a loved one ward off the fear of death when they express the wish not for ending life but for its new and perfect beginning in heaven, paradise, or other idealized forms of the afterlife. These fantasized reunions with the idealized initial state of existence may involve regression to early states where there is little differentiation between self and object, where there is a significant loss of objective reality testing, and where animistic, magical thinking predominates. Pollock (1975) says that most conceptions of heaven, paradise, and the ideal state of afterlife imply a regression to a beginning state of symbiosis and provide the basis for the belief in immortality. Such conceptions also include fantasies of rejoining the dead via a symbiotic reunion with a figure, nonspecific as to gender, who represents the first omnipotent, omniscient parent, or maternal being. Paradoxically, then, symbiotic fantasies of dying or killing oneself ward off the fear of death, for they express the wish not for ending life, but for its new and perfect beginning. Pollock thus provides a helpful understanding of Liebestod fantasies, although he does not refer to them by that name.

Idyllic reunion fantasies (Blatt 1978) and the yearning for the Garden of Eden or of Paradise Lost, however, may also have adaptive, survival value. Structurally speaking, these fantasies may coexist with a very high level of certain ego functions, even though reality testing may be suspended, if only temporarily. The state of being-in-love as evocative of blissful symbiosis is not solely a regressed fusion state but is an alteration in the state of consciousness based on variations in ego functioning. When that functioning is pathological, the yearnings may burst forth in a suicidal or murderous outcome of the fatal attractions of the Liebestod.

It is important to note some of the conditions in which passionate involvement would not necessarily cancel out ego functioning and regard for the object and the self. For one, intense passions need not seek outlet only in "eternal" relationships where there is no letup in intensity and no opportunity for the ego to resume its mastery of the drives. For another, the passion which de Rougemont sees as culminating in literal death culminates, normally, in what Bak (1973) characterizes as the "death from which one returns to life, 'le petit mort.' " The altered ego state of orgasm thereby gratifies and renews regularly the need for the intensity of a grand passion, the temporary suspension of many ego functions, and a living out of the fantasy of death through reunion and the ever-returning illusion of immortality and blissful merger.

Falling-in-love, or being-in-love, then, can be a *capacity* of the ego, and not, per se, a pathological aberration. This capacity is not only compatible with a loving concern for the object, but is an important step toward the development of object constancy in rich and full total relationships. Pathological symbiosis, boundary fusion and blinding idealization in troublesome being-in-love states could lead to such pathological outcomes as the implied suicide pacts of the Tristan legend and the overt ones in its contemporary versions. Normal being-in-love, when there is full separation-individuation, boundary-crossing, and flexibility in ego functioning could lead to positive outcomes of Liebestod fantasies, such as object love and creative mastery of fatalism. The distinction I propose is reminiscent of the distinction between mourning and melancholia, in that the grief of mourning reflects ego adaptation and the despair of melancholia, ego regression. So we come full circle from contemporary psychoanalysis back to Freud's (1917) original thoughts on these matters.

If we look at the differential outcomes of Liebestod fantasies following significant loss in the autobiographical accounts of Sylvia Plath and the psychoanalyst, George Engel, we shall see that a crucial factor in the mastery of fatalism lies in the capacity to deal effectively with the experience of loss. Engel (1975) wrote of how he began to succumb to suicidal impulses when he nearly expired by neglecting his health following the death of a twin brother with whom he intimately identified. Plath failed at this task of mastery, whereas Engel succeeded by means of a rigorous self-analysis. Now why is this so? Clearly, there are certain individuals whose early and continuously activated losses have left them more vulnerable than others to that kind of loss of self and object differentiation which can end with the extinction of the self via literal death. The subjective experience of the fusion of self and object representations is an alteration of the sense of reality, at times a depersonalization. Engel tells us that this form of ego regression may have ominous conse-quences when it represents an untempered longing for symbiosis or dedifferentiation, that is, untempered by the drive toward separate-ness and individuation. In such a psychic situation, even though there is no wish for literal death but only for reunion with a loved one, the consequences may be literally lethal.

Even under the most traumatic conditions, however, there seems to be an adaptive potential for self-realization through creative mastery. Engel reports that he was aware that the very act of writing up his experience was part of the mourning process, itself, and was also a creative transformation of narcissism. That is, the creative act of mastering a loss through writing about it reestablishes the tie with the object, an object which is a selfobject as well as a libidinal object. So, in Kohut's (1971) terms, writing about it or in other ways articulating and understanding one's own experience of loss and dedifferentiation is a creative transformation of narcissism through coming to terms with one's own mortality.

Sylvia Plath also had her creative periods to mourn her father's death. Alvarez tells us of them: "In the dead hours between night and day, she was able to gather herself in silence and isolation, almost as though she were reclaiming some past innocence and freedom before life got a grip on her" (1971, 37). Tragically, the reclamation effect had its limits.

The creative mastery through art, if one is talented, might also be regarded as a recovery or refinding of the irretrievably lost object via the creative fantasy of a substitute or surrogate. Our pathographic reading of Wagner's repeated use of the love-death and reunion theme in his operas could lead us to view it as a creative transformation of the composer's real-life conflicts, whereby the actual fatal tragedy of the Liebestod was averted. The ultimate aim of many creative artists is to conquer the fear of death and to achieve immortality. The subject of immortality thus heralds part 2 of this book, which will deal with the topic of resurrection fantasies.

The Pathological and the Normal in Fantasies of Merger and Symbiosis

The fantasies of symbiotic reunion underlying the Liebestod are a good case in point for sorting out the pathological from the normal. In the illustrations of symbiotic reunion fantasies that follow, both ends of the spectrum are well represented. Bergmann (1971) states that the Liebestod in the great love stories is chosen in preference to separation and is a poetic rendering of the emotions that belong to the symbiotic phase when separation means death. Because love revives emotions that once belonged to the symbiotic phase, it is often feared as endangering the boundary of the self.

An example of the Liebestod in preference to separation occurs in *Die Walküre,* when Siegmund rejects the delights of Valhalla because his twin sister, Sieglinde, will not be permitted to accompany him there. *Siegmund is determined, now that he knows that his own death is inevitable, to kill Sieglinde rather than leave her to face life alone.* It is Brünnhilde in *Götterdämmerung* who, as we recall, entertained murderous wishes, when she believed that Siegfried had betrayed her. In the former opera, which takes place earlier in the Ring Cycle and before Siegfried's birth, she condemns Siegmund to leave Sieglinde and seek safety in Valhalla when she hears tidings that Siegmund is marked for death:

> Here on earth
> you have to leave her:
> Sieglinde sees Siegmund no more. (John 1983, 87)

Siegmund, however, wishes to die with Sieglinde rather than go to Valhalla, as expressed in the Liebestod lines,

> So long as she lives
> I'll allow no other to touch her:
> if I have to die, I will kill her first while she sleeps. (87)

Knowing now that the sword, Notung, having had its magic powers removed by Wotan, will fail him in his fight with Sieglinde's husband, Hunding, Siegmund decides,

> since it must fail on my foe, I'll use it instead on a friend.
> Two lives now lie in your power;
> take them Notung,
> glittering blade
> Two within a single stroke. (88)

Sieglinde now joins actively in the love-death scenario:

> Stop the fight, you madmen!
> Murder me first! (89)

When Wotan takes away Notung's power and Siegmund falls dead to the ground, Sieglinde, who has heard his death-sigh, falls with a cry, as if lifeless, to the ground. Hunding falls dead, too. Brünnhilde, at the ready, does not permit Sieglinde to die, knowing she is pregnant with Siegmund's son. But Sieglinde is not grateful for her compassion, craving instead the Liebestod over separation:

> Pray suffer no sorrow for me;
> all I long for is death!
> O warrior maid,
> who asked you to save me?
> I might have died in the field with him;
> for perhaps the weapon
> that dealt his death
> that killed my Siegmund
> had pierced me too.
> Far from Siegmund,
> Siegmund from you!
> *Now only death can unite us!*
> *So I shall curse*
> *this care that has saved me*
> *if you refuse my grievous entreaty*
> *strike with your sword in my heart!* (96 [italics mine])

But Sieglinde quickly changes her mind about wanting a violent death by being murdered, or wanting to die at all, for that matter, as she learns from Brünnhilde that a Wälsung, Siegmund's child from their joint blood line, lives in her womb. She implores of the Valkieries:

> Save me, you maidens,
> and shelter my son! . . .
> Rescue me, maid!
> Rescue a mother! (97)

So, in *Die Walküre*, the Liebestod is sacrificed for another form of reunion, the symbiotic reunion of mother with her own child, more convincing evidence for Bergmann's point that the Liebestod is chosen in preference to separation. When it is clear that separation is to be avoided through promised reunion with the next generation of her own and Siegmund's incestuous blood tie, we note a reversal of

Bergmann's observation: rather than being chosen in preference to separation, the Liebestod is given up in preference for the anticipated symbiotic reunion. This reversal is assumed, psychoanalytically speaking, to be a confirmation of the very point it appears to negate. It is not the "bad death" of suicide and murder nor the "good death" of reunion that is yearned for. Reunion is yearned for by continuing life and not at all through death. This transformation represents a movement from the pathological to the normal. Since murderous wishes are involved in the Liebestod examples cited, we need to assess the relative degrees of normality and pathology of the wish to avoid separation and aloneness with its accompanying "good" and "bad" death wishes.

The hypothesis of Liebestod fantasies as derivative of the symbiotic phase is an intriguing one. Because affects deriving from early symbiosis and fusion are evocative of the love-death aspects of being-in-love, some adults fear the altered state of consciousness and the sexual passion and other intense feelings that being-in-love brings about, because these alterations threaten their sense of separateness and integrity of the self. These feelings and fears may evoke fantasies and dim, repressed memories of having "experienced" engulfment and merger, but they do not revive the early ego states exclusively. Oedipal pressures, frustrations, and anxieties may be responsible for fear of loving, serving as a warning signal for regression to early ego states. The resultant "state" in the adult, however, is far more complex than a simple revival of the infantile symbiotic state. Bergmann (1980) rightly says that the state of symbiosis in being-in-love is a state sui generis: it is neither regressive nor pathological per se. That is, there simply may be temporary suspension of certain ego functions, analogous to creative or "controlled" regressions. In such instances, being-in-love in and of itself does not necessarily preclude a loving concern for the object, although it may. When it does, we are dealing with a condition that appears to characterize the relationships depicted in many of the great romantic love stories.

Freud (1914) said that a "real happy love corresponds to the primal condition in which object-libido and ego-libido cannot be distinguished" (100). That is, in a state of being-in-love, one loves the object as if he or she were oneself. It does not seem quite right, however, to say that a *correspondence* to the original state of primary narcissism implies a revival of only that state, nor is any significant self and object dedifferentiation implied. Too much has intervened developmentally. It seems, too, that Freud was not referring as much to "boundary fusion" as he was to identification—especially to cross-identifications and the interchanging of identifications. The process of identification is pivotal to an understanding of being-in-love and loving, for it subsumes a hierarchy of experiences originating in the subjective sense of merging and then proceeding upward through a differentiated capacity for empathy.

Pathological identification with one who has died, or one with whom one wishes to die, is a concept that has been used to explain those variants of the Liebestod in which there is either a suicide pact or a suicide-murder pact. The mechanism of pathological identification may be broken down into its more familiar components of wishes to die and reunite, of self-neglect in the service of realizing a fantasy, and introjection of an ambivalently loved figure of great importance. The fear of getting too close in relationships, the fear of becoming engulfed or of psychic death, is only the other side of the coin of the wish to die together in timeless death. The latter, as one more example of the yearned-for "good death" is to be found in the closing lines of the Liebestod love duet that ends the opera, *Siegfried*, where laughter and happiness characterize the love-death yearnings:

> BRÜNNHILDE:
> By the heat of my blood
> in its passionate surge
> a fire is kindled
> can you not feel?
> Tell me then, Siegfried,
> do you not fear
> this wild passionate maid?
> . . . laughing, welcome my blindness
> *laughing, let us be lost together*
> *in laughter die*

SIEGFRIED:
Light of our loving
laughter in death (John 1984, 57 [italics mine])

It is of greatest importance to emphasize that *fantasies* of rejoining are not to be equated with the *experience* of symbiotic merger, even though, in dreaming or dreamlike states, they may revive certain dim memories and impressions of early states. This formulation is consistent with those of Isakower (1938) and Lewin (1946), who stay close to the clinical data of dreams and sensations of adult patients. Their formulations do not confuse these clinical data with the data gleaned from infant observations. Pollock (1975), too, appears to refer not to literal revival of archaic infantile ego states but rather to internalized ideals and object representations, to later developed and elaborated fantasies about what intrauterine life, or early oral symbiosis, must have been like.

The important phenomenon of idealization often reflects merger, bliss, or symbiosis fantasies. At the height of the normal being-in-love state, as at the height of sexual passion with its attendant normal idealization of the love object, the boundary between ego and object threatens to "melt away." In Kohut's terms (1971), the love-object becomes the idealized selfobject. In Freud's terms, ego libido and object libido cannot be distinguished. Freud (1930) also said, "Against all the evidence of his senses, a man who is in love declares that 'I' and 'you' are one, and is prepared to behave as if it were a fact" (66). Idealization of the loved object occurs, said Freud, because the lover tends to see in the object the image of some *previously* loved person, who, by means of nostalgic revisions of early memories, becomes loved unambivalently. The loved object is thus overestimated and romanticized as perfect. The condition of "normal" romantic love, then, is *not* a symbiotic regression, although it involves the investment of a considerable quality of narcissistic libido in the object who then replaces the ego ideal.

Symbiosis, a potentially serious regression in any adult, may be conceptualized as psychological death insofar as it precludes separateness and the normal development of various ego functions. Paralleling the normal and pathological modes of recapturing symbiotic representations in the being-in-love state are normal and pathological modes of achieving separateness and individuation. The prototypical pathological modes are beautifully illustrated by Tristan's driven and repetitive adventures and escapes which have a life-or-death quality to them. People who seek out such trials and ordeals are not simply exercising the autonomous functions of the ego in their adventures but often are enacting maladaptive repetitive patterns of avoidance and escape from the feared subjective experience of the engulfment state. The alternation, or fragmentation, of seeking merger during heightened passion and fighting off commitment and engulfment fears by exaggerated self-sufficiency and efforts to achieve autonomy in ways that to the casual observer appear masochistically self-defeating are the hallmark of unresolved preoedipal conflicts.

Pathological being-in-love and normal being-in-love can be distinguished in terms of the level of ego functioning that accompanies the passionate state. The pathological is characterized by boundary fusions, pathological identifications and maladaptive or uncontrolled ego regressions. The normal is characterized by full separation-individuation, boundary crossing, and flexibility in ego functioning despite longer or shorter moments of what, if characterological, would be considered pathological. This distinction is crucial for understanding the outcome of Liebestod fantasies, whether they eventuate in real or symbolic death, e.g., a suicide pact, as in the Tristan legend, or whether they lead to creative mastery and object love. The troubadours tell us that romantic love is inevitably blind, and that because it blinds judgment, anticipation, and routine reality contact, what psychoanalysts designate as ego functions, it can survive only in a passionate state, one which, in this context, sounds split off, fragmented, or dissociated. The sometimes seemingly irreconcilable split between being-in-love and loving represents a more pathological than normal state of affairs, for normally, passion necessitates a relation to an object, a relation that implies the ego's capacity to respond to the realities of the object. Normally the two states, passion on the one hand, and reality testing or object constancy on the other, alternate or blend. There are moments when one or the other state predominates and their reconciliation is achieved when the level of the ego's functioning oscillates between controlled regressions and adaptation.

Conclusion

The relation between loving, being-in-love, and passion has rarely been thought out in psychoanalysis. Winnicott (1958), however, has come very close to an appreciation of important distinctions when he contrasts the quiet loving and liking of "ego-relatedness" with the more passionate loving of "id-relatedness." It is possible, says Winnicott, that "id relationships strengthen the ego when they occur in a framework of ego relatedness" (34).

The polarization between passion and loving concern for the object should be regarded as a split or fragmentation into two or more relationships of something that cannot be managed within one. Intense passions, however, need not seek outlet only in "eternal" relationships where there is no letup in intensity and no opportunity for the ego to regain its equilibrium and resume mastery of the drives. Passion, as I noted earlier, usually culminates in that "death" from which one returns to life, *"le petit mort."* The altered ego state of orgasm gratifies and renews regularly the needs for the intensity of a grand passion, the temporary suspension of many ego functions and a living out of the fantasy of death through reunion via the ever-returning illusion of immortality and blissful merger. The passion with which Tristan loves, in contrast, is savored for its own sake, and is heightened to a painful intensity of sentiment, indifferent to its living and external object. It is no accident that we know virtually nothing about Iseult as a real person over and above the cultural and narrative conventions of the time in which women in literature were rarely, if ever, more than objects.

My main point here is that passion, in and of itself, is neither pathological nor adaptive. It may or may not escalate into sadomasochism or "lethal" narcissistic indulgence at the expense of self-regard and regard for the object. It may be considered pathological when critical ego functions, such as reality testing or object constancy do not coexist or reliably alternate with it. Thus, from the side of the ego, as in the development of the capacity for loving, there is hope for lovers that they may enjoy the intensity of passion and being-in-love (the narcissistic-libidinal cathexis) while at the same time preserving the object-relatedness of loving (the object-libidinal cathexis).

This integrative position is consistent with Freud's point that "the finding of an object is in fact a refinding of it" (1905, 222). This refinding could now be understood as a rapprochement between nostalgic idealization and object constancy in love relationships. Bergmann (1971) states that certain ego functions, such as reality testing, must be temporarily suspended if the necessary idealization prerequisite to the capacity to fall in love is to take place. Yet he says, paradoxically, this very reality-testing function must be simultaneously operative to make possible the selection of a good mate. The apparent paradox may be resolved by noting that the ego may maintain an equilibrium, oscillating in all its functions, variably, in levels of regression, adaptation, or dominance. As Bergmann so rightly emphasized, when falling-in-love or being-in-love reflects a capacity of the ego and not some pathological aberration, it is compatible with the development of object constancy and with loving concern for the object.

The study of the prototypical Liebestod legend of Tristan and Iseult, and of others like it, in terms of the multiple fantasies they might embody, adds to our understanding of the psychology of love. In chapter 1, I delineated, via allusion to the Tristan legend, the romantic-erotic conditions sometimes involved in creativity. In chapters 2 and 3, I have approached the question of love from another direction and have tried to delineate the creative-adaptive conditions required for integrating the experiences of loving and being-in-love. I have highlighted the contrasting pathological states when some of the necessary conditions are taken to extremes. This chapter has developed and summarized my main thesis of a continuum of normal and pathological influences on romantic love-death fantasies. The "high tale of love and death," the Liebestod fantasy realized, is still with us, but the happier ending may be a realistic, viable alternative.

Part Two

Resurrection Fantasies

Four

Resurrection Themes: An Introduction

*T*he connection between resurrection themes and romantic love is elucidated when we discover that certain fantasies of resurrection contain ideas of sensual happiness after death, as in the condensation of Liebestod and Resurrection motifs in "le petit mort" of orgasm. The feelings of dying and merger that accompany the sexual climax are certainly to be understood as occurring within the normal range of psychic phenomena. It should become clear that resurrection fantasies, like Liebestod fantasies, span the range from the normal through the pathological. In the wish for a "good death," a point of confluence can be found for themes of fatality and reunion in the Liebestod, and for fantasies of one's own immortality via resurrection. Donald Henahan (1990), writing for the *New York Times* on October 21, 1990, on the death of Leonard Bernstein, surely grasped the essence of this nexus in illustrating how the conductor-composer dramatized his life in neo-Wagnerian terms. Like his idol, Gustav Mahler, Bernstein remained in the grip of an obsession with love and death. Henahan, noting that Mahler's *Resurrection Symphony* was a favorite of Bernstein, concluded that "for both men, the most appropriate funeral music might be the Liebestod." The notion of reunion via resurrection includes hopes, intrinsic in the Liebestod, of perpetual eroticism and ecstasy of love after death, as well as hopes for symbiotic merger and fusion; Liebestod fantasies of dying together include hopes of resurrecting the love relationship after death.

Part 2 of this book presents a psychoanalytic elaboration of resurrection symbolism as it appears in art and life, and the interface of the two realms. Approaching the theme of resurrection, interpretively, from the vantage point of classical legend, theology, and iconography, particularly in its explicit images in the Italian and Northern Renaissance paintings and sculpture of the Christ story, can illuminate the unconscious meanings of patients' resurrection fantasies. Approaching the task from the other direction, a psychoanalytic understanding of the resurrection fantasies of patients should be able to expand the context for our understanding and interpretation of certain latent meanings in works of art in which the manifest content is that of resurrection.

I shall conclude my presentation with some clinical material from the analysis of an older patient, a man whose life's leitmotif could be characterized as a compulsive quest for sexual encounters in an effort to prolong his life indefinitely. His drivenness to find love, always with a counterpoint of preoccupation with his own death, will be shown to be a form of "fatal attraction," an example of the clinically pathological. His work, which happens to be surgery, can be studied with a focus analogous to the thematic, pathographic method, that is, by tracing a theme in the life of the individual whose work is being studied (see Spitz 1985). Themes of resurrection will be shown to appear with considerable regularity in the handiwork of his avocational pursuits, which include fine art appreciation, collecting of archaeological objects, restoration of antiques, gardening, carving, and whittling. The patient is of particular interest because not only were fantasies of resurrection uncommonly prominent in his analysis but he was himself a "would-be-artist" and well acquainted with immortality themes in art and literature. In his rich, inner fantasy life, we will also find aspirations, indeed painful obsessions, to guarantee the permanency of his own handiwork, as well as dreams of creating great masterpieces of wide renown. He believed that the works, by being resurrected after his death, could assure his immortality, and he unconsciously fantasized that they would assure his own bodily resurrection of the flesh, as well. In focusing on normal and pathological aspects of resurrection fantasies, I shall stress the distinctions in ego functioning in the normal and pathological narcissism that characterize the form that resurrection concerns may take.

Now that we are seeing in analysis more and more people who have entered their sixth, seventh, and eighth decades, it is not at all uncommon to observe manifest concerns about death along with immortality fantasies, of which a resurrection fantasy is a frequently encountered variation. A "resurrection fantasy" appeared so impressively and repetitively in the late-middle-aged analysand whom I shall be discussing that as I began to ponder the various unconscious meanings I was able to uncover, it seemed to me that the concerns of my patient, in both their normal and pathological aspects, might be encountered rather frequently in a typical practice and I wondered why there is so little in the psychoanalytic literature on this subject. I could find the word "resurrection" in only one title (Blacker 1983) and its explicit appearance in very few texts (Bak 1973; Edelheit 1974; Lifton 1979; Liebert 1983; Kaplan 1991). The theme is given its most extensive treatment by Leo Steinberg (1983), an art historian who is very ambivalent about psychoanalytic interpretations of art, in his "tour de force," *The Sexuality of Christ in Renaissance Art and in Modern Oblivion.* The general idea of resurrection *may* be inferred from, although not very specifically dealt with in, only a sprinkling of other psychoanalytic works (Freud 1911, 1915, 1926; Lewin 1950). Moreover, the idea of resurrection is not even hinted at in Freud's (1923) best-known discussion of death fears and their unconscious meanings. However, if we turn to art and to literature, particularly to classical mythology and Christian iconography (Panofsky 1939; Grabar 1968; Hall 1974; Sill 1975), we come across an array of riches that can be mined with a dazzling psychoanalytic yield.

A confluence of Liebestod and resurrection symbolism, familiar to all students of and participants in passionate love, is to be found in the image of the red rose and the green briar entwined in a true lovers' knot, commemorating the death and then the resurrection of two who have loved and died. Psychoanalysis is familiar with the equation of death and reunion, and might even identify an implicit resurrection mythology embodying fantasies of reunion, or merger, upon dying, with lost objects of childhood. These may be the preoedipal mother, the father of the preoedipal phase who may be fused with the preoedipal mother, or even the oedipal parent of the opposite sex. However, this matter has not received much emphasis in the psychoanalytic literature. Thus, the longed-for object in a resurrection fantasy may be heterosexual or homosexual. Edelheit (1974) notes legendary references to both preferences:

> Oedipus kills his father, marries his mother, and at the end of his life is transfigured and descends bodily into (mother) earth. Christ, on the other hand, renounces his mother ("Woman, what have I to do with thee?" *John*, 4:2) and after his death is resurrected and ascends bodily to join his father in heaven. (195)

Yet, some aspects and versions of the Christ story emphasize reunion with the mother, especially those which have Christ reunited by marriage with his virgin mother, Mary, after his resurrection and her assumption to heaven (see Warner 1976). However, the important father-and-son reunion theme of the Christ story with its negative oedipal implications is the one elaborated most extensively in Renaissance art. The resurrection sculptures of Michelangelo, in particular, suggest Christ's longing for reunion with the father.

A confluence of Liebestod and resurrection fantasies may be discerned in Dante's dream (1294) of Beatrice's death (see figure 2). Beatrice is like Christ. She comes from heaven to earth, takes on flesh, dies, and ascends into heaven. Anguished, Dante is overcome by the urge to die, to join her, and for her to descend to be his guide in the new life.

When there is no confluence of resurrection and Liebestod motifs, we are not dealing with an expression of a wish for a certain type of object love in merger but primarily with a wish for narcissistically continuing the self without particular reference to an object. These differences in relevant ego functions in Liebestod and resurrection fantasies shall constitute the critical bases for differentiating the normal from the pathological in both forms of love-death fantasy.

The Confluence of Liebestod and Resurrection Themes in Wagner's Operas

Wagner's Ring Cycle operas serve well as a bridge or transition from part 1 of this book, on Liebestod fantasies, to this present section on resurrection fantasies. In all four operas of Wagner's Ring Cycle, *Das Rheingold, Die Walküre, Siegfried,* and *Götterdämmerung,* the confluence of Liebestod and resurrection fantasies is to be found in abundance. Starting with the annunciation of death themes in *Siegfried,* we can observe the confluence of Liebestod and resurrection fantasies in a single artistic theme, the endless sleep, always a metaphor for death, and then the awakening of Brünnhilde which coincides with her love-death reunion with Siegfried. At the end of the opera, Brünnhilde is condemned to sleep, defenseless, until the man who loves her wakens her:

> In long deep sleep
> you shall be bound
> the man who wakes you again
> that man awakes you as wife. (John 1985, 106)

This resurrection via breathing the breath of life through love is a version of the Sleeping Beauty fairy tale, for it has the earmarks of a "reverse Liebestod," that is, a craving *to be awakened* and resurrected from a death-like sleep for the purposes of reunion with a lover. The sleeping-beauty image is common in medieval art and also appears in transformed renditions in the nineteenth-century romanticism of the English Pre-Raphaelite paintings. According to Binion (1993), images of sleep and deathliness competed for sex in this genre and he noted how the English painters excelled at portraying titillating torpidity, prime among them Sir Edward Burne-Jones's images of sleeping beauties (see figure 7). His sleeping princess is "stretched out as if in state" (9). In fact, the composition suggests the traditional iconography of the entombed Christ prior to resurrection,

Figure 7. In a reverse Liebestod, the Sleeping Beauty yearns to be awakened and resurrected from a death-like sleep by her lover. (Sir Edward Burne-Jones, *The Sleeping Princess* [1870–90]. Faringdon, Buscot, Oxfordshire. Bridgeman/Art Resource, New York.)

with the guards asleep at their task. The manifest content in the wish to be awakened, psychoanalytically speaking, reflects the opposite latent wish *to die* in order to reunite. Note the similarity in composition to Burne-Jones's dead King Arthur (figure 16). Symmetry in opposition of manifest content almost always implies identity in the latent meaning of the wish. In fact, when the sleeping beauty Brünnhilde of Norse myth and romantic opera awakens to Siegfried's embrace, she loses her divinity and becomes human. The sequence of events of the Norse goddess as sleeping beauty is exactly the reverse of those in the life of Christ, who was the human Jesus, transfigured into God in his resurrection.[1]

> Wotan then
> dealt with the maid
> and he closed her eyelids in sleep
> on that rock asleep she lies
> That holy maid
> can be wakened alone
> roused by some man who makes her his bride. (John 1984, 110)

The word, rouse, contains an obvious double entendre, meaning both sexual arousal and arousal from either sleep or death, a condensation that found expression in the earlier literary history of the Italian Renaissance in Boccaccio's (1350a, 1350b) punning connection of the novitiate monk Rustico's arousal of the flesh with Christ's rising in his resurrection. This connection between the sacred and the profane, if you will, documents Steinberg's erection-resurrection equation (1983), to be discussed in chapter 5 in the sections dealing with the sexual innuendoes underlying the Christian theological emphasis on the resurrection of the flesh.

One might say that Brünnhilde's death for the love of a man, her endless sleep, ends in life, whereas Siegfried's life for the love of woman ends in death. Although the resurrection motif predominates in the case of Brünnhilde, and the Liebestod for Siegfried, the two are not so different and are intrinsically interrelated, at least in this work.

> My sleep is at an end
> awake I see

> Siegfried! Siegfried
> has brought me to life. (John 1984, 119)

In the final opera of the Ring Cycle, *Götterdämmerung*, the confluence of Liebestod and resurrection motifs is most apparent. In an
introductory commentary to the Porter translation (John 1985) of
the opera, Christopher Wintle refers to the protagonists' preoccupation with a need to regain a lost Eden (Valhalla): "Everyone lives
under the shadow of a prophetic determinism that is as inexorable as
it is apocalyptic" (21). Wintle sees the opera as representing Wagner's
mythic dreams which he believes testify to the quasi-religious, re-
demptive, apocalyptic aspirations of a suffering humanity. In this, as
in all apocalyptic variants of resurrection themes, prominent attention is paid to the hopes of rebirth through regaining Eden, or
Heaven, after the doom. Valhalla, in *Götterdämmerung*, represents
in part an attempt to retrieve a lost paradise. Siegfried regains paradise by celebrating his consummate love for Brünnhilde. The opera,
then, belongs in that category of resurrection fantasy that is an
apocalyptic story of the resurrection of the dead and the regaining of
Paradise Lost. Siegfried, while on his own funeral pyre, radiantly
entreats Brünnhilde to awake from her slumber, to resurrect, as it
were, and only then does he die in peace. In what easily could be
identified as the Liebestod of this opera, Brünnhilde oversees the
building of Siegfried's funeral pyre:

> Kindle the flame
>   let the hero blaze
> in splendour and radiance on high
> His horse bring to my side
> he and I together must join him
>   I shall share that pure, holy flame
>   with the hero
> we both shall blaze in the fire. (John 1985, 121–22)

Then, as the fire consumes both Siegfried and Brünnhilde, Brünnhilde
returns the ring to the Rhinemaidens swimming in the deep. With her
complete humanation comes a Liebestod motif indistinguishable
from that of resurrection, as she leads her horse into the flames with

all the yearnings of the Liebestod, consummating in her desire for eternal reunion with her lover:

> In fiery glory
> blazes your lord
> Siegfried my hero and love
> . . . .
> Lured by the fire,
> the light and its laughter?
> I too am yearning
> to join him there;
> glorious radiance
> has seized in my heart.
> I shall embrace him
> united with him
> in sacred yearning
> with him ever one!
> . . . .
> Brünnhilde greets you as wife! (John 1985, 124)

Thus the final opera of the cycle ends. Although the opera's major theme is that of redemption, the focus on life beyond death falls into the broad category of resurrection. Brünnhilde ecstatically leaps astride her horse onto the life-consuming fire of Siegfried's funeral pyre, exclaiming her wishes to embrace him, to wed him, to die with him in an eternal love-death all at once. Death, for Brünnhilde in her transports, as the cardinal sign of humanation, would seem to be the only means of attaining the ultimate: peace and love, reserved for mortals, denied to the gods. Her enactment of a Liebestod fantasy in her leap into fire—which symbolizes the consummation of erotic passion as much as it symbolizes the final consummation of life—is delusional and ecstatic in its joyful embrace of annihilation together as a continuation in the afterlife of life's joyous erotic pleasures. Her apparent folly screams out her fundamental yearning not to exist, that is, to be a mortal with the hope for eternal love in life after death rather than an immortal god, deprived of the pains and pleasures of human flesh, of love, and of final peace through death.

The irony, of course, is that notions of death in resurrection fantasies such as these do not rule out notions of ecstatic bliss, viewable as the opposite of a peaceful, tensionless state. Contradictory wishes may indeed exist side by side in the metaphorical unconscious. In his introduction to the Porter translation, Tanner (1985) discusses Brünnhilde's ecstasy in dying and notes that Wagner's characters are always in search of peace, yet

> at the same time have such stamina that only the most shattering experiences can bring them to their deaths. One of the fascinations we find in them, as indeed in their creator, is that they shirk no ordeals in seeking to fulfill themselves. Like the Virgin in Titian's great painting of the Assumption in Venice, which Wagner found such an inspiration, who is "borne aloft by the fullness of life that is within her" [Berenson's words] they naturally live and die in a state of ecstasy. (11)

Once again, "'tis yearning and dying," as the motif of the Tristan legend leaps out at us, with the additional ideas of consummation of love and purification of souls. The fire that kindles love as it melts the lovers together in death is the setting for a Liebestod reunion that holds the promise of eternal embrace in the afterlife. In the ecstatic sexual consummation in death, the lovers are consumed. The yearnings simultaneously are the wish for a grand sexual climax that continues in perpetuity and the wish for peaceful, tensionless merger in eternal sleep. The rendition of immortality themes in grand opera itself survives through the generations with the longevity of the opera's life. The operatic work, fated itself to be immortal, realizes the wishes and fantasies underlying the themes it has so magnificently expressed, particularly the wish for immortality of the ego. If the sexual aspects of resurrection were treated directly instead of by symbolic substitution, as in Steinberg's erection-resurrection equation, we would be dealing with a vulgarization or contamination of love-death mythology. By casting the sexual and "mundane" aspects into the more transcendental realm of art forms, such as Norse myths, the New Testament, Renaissance art, and romantic opera, the passionate themes are preserved in a form palatable and appealing to universal tastes and longings. The form in which the art is contained resonates with the psyche.

∼

I turn now from the normative to the more pathological confluence of Liebestod and resurrection fantasies. Louise Kaplan (1991)
in her account of female perversions has been one of the few psychoanalytic thinkers to make explicit reference to resurrection. In her
ever-recurring refrain, Kaplan characterizes elements of numerous
perverse scenarios as representing "abandonment and reunion, castration and reparation, death and resurrection" (143). The scenario
she regards as expressing the quintessential female perversion, also
seen in men but not as typically, involves abject submission, similar
to that found in pathological Liebestod variants. For example, in a
typical female perversion

> The woman allows herself to be lowered to a state of abject humilia-
> tion, despair, and panic so that she can be *resurrected to a state of
> sexual ecstasy*. By granting and withholding his penis, the man enables
> and facilitates these cycles of *castration and restitution, abandonment
> and mystical reunion, death and resurrection*. (217 [italics mine])

In the typical love songs of the medieval troubadours, a male perversion is central: the man is the lover, abjectly adoring the unattainable
femme fatale. Such a relationship was found in Petrarch's love for
Laura, Dante's for Beatrice. Kaplan adds the female counterpart,
summarizing both a female and a male version of what the reader
might now identify as the erection-resurrection equation as it appears
in sexual perversions: "Perverse performances are about desperate
need. The actresses and actors are using penises and vaginas as
instruments for playing out the repetitive cycle of *castration and
restitution, abandonment and reunion, death and resurrection*" (218
[italics mine]). In the female version, according to Kaplan, the slave
of love is seeking castration, abandonment, and death through the
medium of love and pleasure. In what she has labelled the *Hörigkeit*
script, after Krafft-Ebbing's 1886 term for sexual bondage or extreme
submissiveness, Kaplan has the perversion-afflicted woman living
only for her moments of "ecstatic *union mystico*" (1991, 215). She
believes that the *Hörigkeit* script, which need not be limited to one

or the other sex exclusively, is about unbearable losses, profound depression, and death. Although Kaplan does not refer specifically to Liebestod fantasies in this connection of sexual submissiveness to bondage in the hopes of ecstatic and grandiose resurrection of the self on the part of woman, she does relate *Hörigkeit* to traditional notions of romantic love. She maintains that extreme submissiveness, accompanied by sexual ecstasies, contains the wish to be awakened or resurrected and

> resembles the more familiar romantic love, which is also an ecstasy of *union mystico,* a sexual passion so intense that it dissolves the boundaries between the lover and the beloved. The difference is, that in a true *aimer d'amour,* the surrender, the mystical union is mutual. . . . The extraordinary romantic surrender of ordinary falling in love becomes a perversion when "the only possible sexual excitement consists in the feeling of one's own insignificance as compared with the magnificence of the loved one." (228)

As noted earlier, the connection between sexual bondage and the Liebestod is well recognized, as in the romantic ideal of the male bondage to the femme fatale. A latter-day version of this typical male perversion is exemplified by the professor in the movie *The Blue Angel.* So men throughout the ages have been portrayed as suffering from the perversion of extreme bondage, ending in suicide, a perversion designed to overcome death fears and eventuate in a hoped-for resurrection. Social and sexual evolution and revolution enable an easier recognition of female perversions which are characterized by extreme sexual bondage to the idealized man, often experienced as the male equivalent of the femme fatale. He is submitted to by that woman whom Kaplan labels the sexually submissive *femme evaporée.* The *femme evaporée* is exemplified by the fictional Emma Bovary:

> Emma was precisely the sort of girl who would linger at the confessional, prolonging the ecstasies inspired by the priest's whispered references to heavenly lovers and eternal marriages. Her eyes feasted on the images of the sick lamb, the Sacred Heart pierced with arrows, and poor Jesus suffering as He stumbled under His cross. (Kaplan 1991, 330–31)

Although Kaplan herself does not make the connection explicit, it seems clear that her selection of this aspect of Emma Bovary's psyche was meant to convey the close connection between Liebestod and Christ's resurrection themes in the love-death imagery of perverse sexual submissiveness. Kaplan argues,

> What has not been sufficiently appreciated is that, like perversion itself, the literature of perversion—pornography—is about death, murder, primitive sadistic aggression, and dehumanization. . . . It is the *public* display of O's body and the reducing of her flesh to a Zero that reveals the death mask grinning behind the mask of love. Our mass media, computerized, consumer sex is a democratized version of the old Roman orgies, which were also celebrations of mutilation and death in the guise of erotic love. (343–44)

Finally, the love-death connection in the perversions is summarized:

> And though the mask of Eros that usually masks the grinning mask of Death is *barely* discernible in the most extreme acts of self-mutilation, there is still an erotic element, still a longing to realize one's illusions of perfection, still a wish to be reunited with some almighty one who gave love and then took it away. (368)

In the examples cited, it is a challenging task to sort out the normal from the pathological. When we consider the joining together of the man who seeks out the femme fatale, and the *femme evaporée* who seeks her magnificent idealized other, we are dealing with pathological love relationships in couples whose jointly held resurrection and Liebestod fantasies motivate their seeking out of particular forms of ecstatic, romantic love. As for the place of love and death in the perversions and in the life of such characters as the fictional Emma Bovary, we are clearly dealing with the pathological end of the spectrum. In such artistic renderings as Wagner's, the symbolic representations of love and death in Liebestod and resurrection covers the range of distinctly human experience. Pathological variants of sadomasochism in the romantic love of the troubadours finds its origin in normal struggles of the preoedipal periods of the comings and goings of the rapprochement crisis. Once again, the universal appeal of the tragic resurrection and redemption themes of the Ring Cycle, like that of the love-death in the Celtic legend of Tristan and Iseult, attests to the normative developmental aspects that of course always have the potential to develop into tragic proportions, with the implied underlying potential for pathological variations on the normal.

Kaplan seems to be suggesting that the loss of ego boundaries in the merger of a perverse Liebestod fantasy is a means toward eventual resurrection through sexual ecstasy. In this sense, she may be describing the female counterpart of the erection-resurrection equation. In the confluence of resurrection and Liebestod fantasies, the loss of ego functioning in the merger of the love-death is a means to achieving what is hoped for in the wish for resurrection: perpetual sexual ecstasy in the afterlife, and the restoration, sometimes via grandiose means, of self expression, of the self that had been lost in the merger of the Liebestod.

Five

Background in Art
and Psychoanalysis

*F*reud's (1911) analysis of Schreber's *Memoirs* is perhaps his only explicit reference to resurrection, clearly in the context of sensual, fatal love. The childless Judge Schreber, in his paranoid delusional system, imagined that a state of perpetual voluptuous bliss would be forthcoming to him if he were reincarnated as a woman to create a new race. Schreber's "state of heavenly bliss is to be understood as being in its essence an intensified continuation of sensual pleasure upon earth!" (29). Schreber's sexualization of the state of heavenly bliss appears, says Freud, to be "derived from a condensation of the two principal meanings of the German word 'selig'—namely, 'dead' and 'sensually happy' " (30). Schreber's resurrection fantasy expresses, among other things, wishes for a state of perpetual sexual arousal, ecstasy, and gratification and suggests a Liebestod motif in the idea of perpetual erection potential to guarantee eternal reunion with a loved one after death. The art historian Leo Steinberg finds this theme so prominent in the images of Renaissance art that he has coined the expression, "erection-resurrection equation" to describe and elaborate the religious meanings underlying these images in his book *The Sexuality of Christ in Renaissance Art and in Modern Oblivion* (1983). In Christian religious tradition, it is, he says, the incarnation of God that underlies the art imagery. He notes that the connection of erection with resurrection predates the art of the Renaissance, going back to antiquity:

> It is not a far cry from one to the other—no straining leap of imagination to equate penile erection, reciprocally, with flesh revivified. . . . As a symbol of postmortem revival, the erection-resurrection equation roots in pre-Christian antiquity: it characterized Osiris, the Egyptian god of the afterlife, represented with his restored member out like a levelled lance. (86)

This juxtaposition of images of human sensuality with those of death and resurrection is pivotal in understanding a most critical nexus for themes of love and death in art and life. The symbolic depictions of the erection-resurrection equation should serve as a splendid starting point for a psychoanalytic exploration of my general topic. Sacrilegious as it may sound, the notion of being sensually happy after death is compatible with the images in Renaissance painting that Steinberg has catalogued, to be reviewed subsequently, of the erect member of the dead Christ. Although this is a connection to be taken seriously, it obviously lends itself to punning, as found in the play on words of Boccaccio. In the Renaissance writer's (1350a, 1350b) famous tenth tale of the third day in *The Decameron,* the young Alibech, in her attempt to do holy deeds, is seduced by Rustico, the novitiate monk, who assures her that the best path to her salvation is "to put the devil back in hell . . . for a great deal can arise and flow in the process." As Rustico convinces her that the act of intercourse is the holiest means to accomplishing this mission, Boccaccio, with great wit and appreciation of this universal symbolic equation tells his punning tale of risen flesh, "la resurrezion della carne." Despite Boccaccio's blasphemous irony, there certainly is an important connection between the ideas of love in life and love after death expressed in this pun that suggests a fantasy of sexual arousal in the resurrection of the flesh following its mortification. The theme of the death of the flesh relates to the narcissistic mortification that some men and women experience or anticipate, particularly as they get older. As Jones (1929) noted, the fear is of *aphanisis,* or the permanent extinction of the capacity for pleasure. These fears are important motivating factors in passionate "fatal" attachments.

Steinberg's erection-resurrection equation is also compatible with the colloquial "le petit mort" for orgasm, and with Elizabethan verse traditions of writing "dying" for orgasm, as swains normally "dye" and "rise." However, its presence across diverse time, cultural, and geographical zones suggests also that the equation derives from reading the works as autonomous texts expressing symbolically disguised universal fantasies of perpetual erection after death. What Steinberg calls an almost banal analogy of erection with resurrection is in fact found beyond the sphere of images of the Christ story across art, literature, and human psychology as a whole, and could find its source in the lives of particular individual artists and poets if we were to apply to their study the pathographic method. The symbolic equation would then have to be understood as expressing more than the Christian theology of the incarnation of God. One universal psychological fantasy it disguises is that of perpetual erection and other forms of sexual pleasure, including ecstatic erotic reunion after death. These resurrection fantasies, along with the symbiotically de-rived wish for the blissful merger of the Liebestod, are central to the quest for fatal attractions. Before returning to the psychoanalytic literature on resurrection fantasies, I should like to review the back-ground of resurrection themes and their various depictions in the field of the arts.

Resurrection Themes in Art

The body of art that is most replete with resurrection themes is the paintings of the Italian and Northern (Flemish) Renaissance. There are two different New Testament Bible stories that inform two dis-tinct but related variations in the well-defined range of resurrection motifs in religious art in the Renaissance. The first is the story of the resurrection of Christ, who rose from the tomb to return to earth on the third day after his death. The second is the story of the Last Judgment, or the Second Coming of Christ, when according to Chris-tian doctrine there will be a general resurrection of all who have ever died and who, along with the living, will be finally judged and assigned to heaven or hell.

To interpret these paintings psychoanalytically, it is important to understand their iconography or the regularities in the traditional ways in which their subject matter is depicted. Iconography, according to Panofsky (1939), includes both the identification of repetitive motifs and the correct analysis of images, stories, and allegories. Most graphic representations in Renaissance paintings of the Resurrection conform to the sequence of events in Christ's life that are recorded in the Gospels as the story of the Passion. The Passion includes his sufferings between the night of the last supper and his death: the flagellation, the crucifixion on Friday, the deposition or pietà, the entombment on Saturday, and the Sunday resurrection. Christ's resurrection is not in fact recorded in the Gospels but is part of the Apostles' creed, "On the third day he rose from the dead." The resurrection marks the beginning of Christ's appearance on earth during the forty days before his ascension to heaven.

In many paintings, Christ is shown rising out of the sarcophagus in a white loincloth surrounded by all of the paraphernalia of the Passion: the ropes, whips, and rods of the flagellation; the crown of thorns; and the objects connected with the crucifixion—the spear that pierced his side and the nails that pinned his hands to the cross. His hands bear the marks of the nails and his right side shows the spear wound from which blood had trickled across to the left side of the body and down to the groin. This blood trickle has been called by Steinberg (1983) the "blood-hyphen," and is featured prominently in his interpretations of Christ's sexuality in resurrection imagery. It is this very iconography that has inspired the interpretive efforts of Steinberg and my own current psychoanalytic exploration.

The classic iconographic representation of the Resurrection, up to the time of the Council of Trent in the middle of the sixteenth century, is of Christ awakening to life, rising from the tomb after forcing open the stone lid that closed the exit from the sepulchral vault. He is holding the flag of the Resurrection, a banner either unadorned or painted with a red cross. The soldiers who have been guarding the tomb look lackadaisical, startled, or frightened. Sometimes they are asleep. Other typical representations, such as Bronzino's *The Descent of the Savior into Limbo* (see figure 8), include sensual images of others who have died and are waiting to be resurrected on Judgment Day. Perugino's 1510 painting *The Resurrection* expresses a typically iconographic theme: Christ is standing on the open tomb, its lid angled off, the banner of the Resurrection held unfurling, the loincloth in parallel fashion unfurling gloriously, the part covering the genitalia painted with visible folds and furls. This latter is particularly noted by Steinberg in his observations of Christ fully risen, erect, and provides fertile soil for developing his theory of linking Christ's resurrection with ideas of erection and incarnation.

The Council of Trent had this traditional iconography censored because it disapproved of the open tomb, thereby resolving a controversy. This censorship was intended to refute the charges of the Jews that the disciples had secretly removed the body. Putting considerations of theological conflict aside for the moment, the censorship imposed by the Church in the sixteenth century can be understood as serving the same function as the censorship resulting from psychological conflict. Ideas about exhumation of bodies carry strong feelings which link to conflictual wishes amenable to psychoanalytic interpretation. The resurrection-related theme of exhuming a corpse in many instances connotes a love theme of wanting a dead lover back *and* of wanting to rejoin a lost one in the grave. Binion (1993) reports how "exhuming a beloved corpse in a paroxysm of grief was common practice pictorially and literally" (14). In the television version of the Gabriel García Márquez and Lisandro Duque screenplay *Miracle in Rome* (1988), for example, a father tenderly watches over the coffin in the crypt that contains the body of his daughter who had died at the age of seven in their home country in Latin America. He exhumes her body years later, finding it completely unchanged, preserved as it was at the time of her death. Interpreting this preservation as a special sign from God, he begins his entreaties to the papal authorities in Rome to recognize this miracle in some official way. The father transports the body to Rome where he negotiates with the papal authorities, and sits by it day and night, waiting for the Vatican's response. In the course of his mission, his beloved daughter, whose

Figure 8. A typical iconographic representation of the resurrected Christ, here in Limbo, with all its sensuality. (Agnolo Bronzino, *The Descent of the Savior into Limbo* [1552]. S. Croce, Florence. Alinari/ Art Resource, New York.)

preserved corpse he lovingly guards in a manner quite unlike the indifferent soldiers guarding Christ's tomb, comes to life. The screenplay ends with the father and daughter reunited, walking away into something like a representation of eternity. The censorship in this realization of a resurrection fantasy is reflected in a plot device in the screenplay: the skepticism of the Church and its resistance to accepting the fact of a beloved daughter's being resurrected as holy, for the purposes of gratifying her father's possibly incestuous wish to rejoin her.

A similar reunion fantasy was found to underlie the dream of a thirty-seven-year-old analysand who had a recurrent dream following the death of her mother. In the dream, the mother appears in the flesh, alive and well, while the daughter asks herself, "How can this be? I was present at the burial as were many others, all of whom bore witness to the fact of death and the fact of the subsequent burial." In the dream itself, the patient ruminates about what could account for this startling and disturbing contradiction of her memories of her experience and concludes that the physician who diagnosed her mother's death must have been mistaken, that she had been buried alive and somehow made her way out of her tomb. In analyzing the dream, it turned out that the patient was expressing a simple reunion fantasy that nonetheless touched on conflict, requiring the dream with its censorship to express the wish. The wish to rejoin her dead mother was repressed during the day for various reasons, among which was the need to disguise her suicidal longings that accompanied the wish to rejoin her mother, longings which were subject to defensive reversal of object and aim in this resurrection dream. It is the mother who rises out of the grave and not the daughter who dies in order to step into it. This clinical vignette illustrates particularly well in a review of the resurrection motifs the close correspondence between resurrection themes in art and life. It underscores the thesis that when universal fantasies inspire outcomes both in paintings and in the dreams of most individuals, we are dealing with the potential normative expression of what could develop into a pathological variant but does not always.

$\sim$

In the iconography of the other category of resurrection imagery, that of the resurrection of the dead, the Last Judgment, or the second coming of Christ, Christ sits on the Throne of Grace. This representation of the end of time is incorporated into paintings, many of which are rendered in a narrative style, telling the story of the apocalypse and the millennium. In these typical Renaissance depictions of Judgment Day, every man and woman who has ever died comes back to life again, rising in their bodies, at age thirty-three, the age at which Christ was believed to have died. In this messianic tale, Christ judges whether they have been good or bad and assigns them a place in heaven or hell for all eternity. In many visual representations, the risen dead first appear as skeletons as they emerge from the cracks of the earth, then as they leave the ground and rise they appear fleshed though naked. Dante's *Inferno* is modeled on this resurrection-of-the-dead theme that is often associated with the Antichrist and other apocalyptic stories of the end of the world. At the crack of doomsday, the Apocalypse, the focus is on the resurrection of the body, usually painted as nude. At the blast of the last trumpet on doomsday, the dead rise, as in Luca Signorelli's famous frescoes in Orvieto. The work as a whole, entitled *Resurrection of the Dead*, contains three frescoes, *The AntiChrist, The End of the World*, and *The Damned*, all expressing apocalyptic themes of prophecies of doom that circulated widely before the year 1500 and the Council of Trent. The figures though are clearly alive, as testified to by the full fleshiness of their nudity (see figure 9), suggesting that the religious censorship of these iconographic representations was motivated by other than theological disputes. The religious censorship influencing iconographic representations in Renaissance art parallel the mind's censorship of sexual material. In many images, the sexuality has been subjected to very little in the way of disguise, achieving full visual juxtaposition with sacred themes. The presence of the sacred themes encourages the viewer to interpret the whole in two disparate ways: as sacrilegious defamation or as constituting a sufficiently diluting or censoring force to mitigate the impact of the sexuality. Like the story

Figure 9. All the dead are resurrected on Judgment Day, in the full fleshiness of their nudity. (Luca Signorelli, *Resurrection of the Dead,* fresco [1499–1502]. Duomo, Orvieto. Alinari/Art Resource, New York.)

of the resurrection of Christ, the story of the resurrection of all the dead finds its counterparts in universal and in idiosyncratic fantasies of a large number of both normal and disturbed individuals in our time and throughout the course of history. Before turning to a fuller consideration of the fantasies and the reason for their disguises in symbol and in dream, I should like to return to the psychoanalytic background literature on resurrection and immortality.

Resurrection Themes in Psychoanalysis

In works subsequent to his specific reference to resurrection in his study of Schreber's paranoid delusions, Freud spoke to the universality of immortality fantasies, if not specifically to fantasies of the resurrection of the flesh. For example, in *Thoughts for the Times on War and Death* (1915) he said, "We would say everyone owed nature a death and is expected to pay the debt. In reality, however, we were accustomed to behave as if it were otherwise" (289). Freud concluded that it is impossible to imagine our own death and that in the unconscious, everyone is convinced of his own immortality:

> It is indeed impossible to imagine our own death; and whenever we attempt to do so we can perceive that we are in fact still present as spectators. Hence the psycho-analytic school could venture on the assertion that at bottom no one believes in his own death, or, to put the same thing another way, that in the unconscious, every one of us is convinced of his own immortality. (289)

Later, Freud (1923, 1926) elaborated his belief that death anxieties cannot be primary but instead covered a more fundamental fear. Because no one can imagine his own death, he concluded that manifest fears of death must signify underlying castration fears:

> These considerations make it possible to regard the fear of death, like the fear of conscience, as a development of the fear of castration. The great significance of which the sense of guilt has in the neuroses makes it conceivable that common neurotic anxiety is reinforced in severe cases by the generating of anxiety between the ego and the super-ego (fear of castration, of conscience, of death). (1923, 58–59)

Freud made a similar point again in 1926, that nothing resembling death has ever been experienced:

> I am therefore inclined to adhere to the view that the fear of death should be regarded as analogous to the fear of castration and that the [danger] situation to which the ego is reacting is one of being abandoned by the protecting super-ego—the powers of destiny—so that it has no longer any safeguard against all the dangers that surround it. (130)

A case arguably can be made that Freud was not quite right in assuming that nothing resembling death has been experienced and that fears of death are always reducible to the four danger situations of childhood. We do fall into deep dreamless sleeps; we lose consciousness under anaesthesia and experience near cessation of stimulation; we wake up after anaesthesia with the sensation of no passage of time; and now, today, we anticipate accurately our cardiac arrests preceding cardiac surgery. We can claim, medically speaking, *that it is possible to die and then come back to life.*

Some considerable time after Freud wrote, this resurrection theme became the subject of a paper by Blacker (1983), "Death, Resurrection, and Rebirth: Observations on Cardiac Surgery," which may be the only psychoanalytic publication to include the term, resurrection, in its title. Blacker states that the direct and real return of the dead to life is a most dramatic form of resurrection. In his paper, he refers to the raising of Lazarus by Jesus, and Jesus' own resurrection as among the most vivid episodes in the Bible, which affirm to the believer the immense power of a god to grant immortality. Blacker presents clinical evidence for a certain present-day version of the resurrection fantasies depicted in the Bible and in Renaissance art, which occurs before and after the resuscitation that follows cardiac arrest. Today, he says, resurrection fantasies have become more common, as the surgical patient has a chance to contemplate his own cardiac arrest and recovery and leisurely to elaborate his fantasies. For the patients whom Blacker has studied, the real occurrence of "death" and resurrection certainly lends a unique stamp to the sense of reality of the resurrection "experience." Blacker presents a case in point, along with others who have reported on various near-death experiences, to question Freud's conviction that nothing resembling death has ever been experienced and therefore death anxieties only symbolize earlier danger situations. According to Blacker, because such patients know there is a good chance for recovery, they *can* contemplate their own deaths and resurrection as real, and thus they provide us with an opportunity to glimpse the formation of a defensive concept of immortality. Blacker reminds us that cardiac standstill is an old medical standard for death; thus, he says, these patients must be regarded as having died and been resurrected, experiencing a unique version of what death and death anxieties are. Their concerns with immortality do indeed appear to be defensive, or as ways of dealing with the prospect of death, and not as Freud believed as a primary conviction of immortality.

Blacker's considerations of a sui generis death experience do not contradict Freud's ideas that the fear of death may also be a fear of castration. In fact, my case material shall illustrate how the two anxiety contents may be condensed. They do give us pause, however, about Freud's suggestions that the manifest fear of death is always and only analogous to the fear of castration and that nothing resembling death has ever been or can be experienced.

In the other psychoanalytic literature after Freud, most of the references to resurrection are, like Freud's, in the context of fantasies of immortality. Bak (1973), however, may have been the first to refer to resurrection fantasies explicitly. Bak believed that the state of suffering from being-in-love serves to undo a prior loss by resurrecting the original object through passionate attachments. He is most interested in

> a case in whose life major turmoils of "being in love" invariably followed significant object loss. . . . These [intensely passionate] object choices and some others were variants of the rescue fantasy. We called it the "resurrection fantasy," because they had the stamp of the adolescent object loss and were characterized by efforts at reviving dead souls or curing the sick by love. (5)

Bak's work on love gets to the heart of the connection between ideas of resurrection and reunion with a lost object. His usage seems derived from those motifs of the resurrection of the dead found in the Bible and graphically depicted in Renaissance art, in which healing and curing of cripples and others are prominent themes. It is also suggestive of Liebestod fantasies that imply a reunion of lovers after death and is an example, such as those found in Wagner's Ring Cycle, of a confluence of Liebestod and resurrection fantasies. He refers to instances that do not highlight the wish to perpetuate the self but to perpetuate the connection with a lost object via resurrection.

Lifton (1979) continues in the tradition of seeing resurrection in the context of immortality and tries to bring us away from a fundamentalist or literal understanding of the afterlife to an appreciation of religious or spiritual achievement, as symbolized, he says, in the Christ story. Although many patients' fantasies are more in keeping with the fundamentalist dogma of life after death, many others do carry the stamp of Lifton's more lofty, humanistic-spiritual aims. Lifton's book focuses in only a minor way on Christian representations of immortality, having as its major emphasis the ancient and the oriental, with only passing reference to the resurrection of Christ. Throughout, Lifton distinguishes between literal and symbolic immortality. The latter, and here he borrows from existential theology, which takes a different view from Freud, suggests an ideal of a mortal being who need not remain numbed toward (ignorant of) the fact of death, yet can transcend it. He also makes specific references to the Liebestod fantasies in *Tristan und Isolde,* where the symbolic as opposed to the literal quality of immortality is expressed as one form of yearning for a continuing connection. Lifton sees these symbolic expressions as positive, humanistic, adaptive aspects of immortality-resurrection concerns. As such they contrast with the pathological aspects of Schreber's delusion and the driven preoccupations of the patient I shall be discussing. For these latter two, ideas of losing the connection with the loved father or with the self as replaced by the child son are expressed through pathological thinking and not, in Lifton's existential terms, a higher order expression of life forces: that is, they do not simply express the normative wish for a continuing connection.

Edelheit (1974), writing of crucifixion fantasies, noted the many themes that embody crucifixion symbolism while also expressing other aspects of human experience embedded in certain times or places. For example, he sees the tradition of crucifixion imagery as expressing primal scene schema, which is also how he sees the typical iconographic depictions of Prometheus, Judith and Holofernes, Abraham and Isaac, St. John at the stake, the bound Gulliver, Snow White, the Sleeping Beauty, Humpty Dumpty, and vampires. "Most of these alternates, like the crucifixion fantasy itself, express the polarities sleeping/waking or death/resurrection" (198). These stories also express other normal and pathological aspects of human experience, such as fantasies of castration, masochistic surrender, and oral incorporation and parthenogenesis.

Psychoanalytic Perspectives on Resurrection Themes in Art and Literature

In the main, resurrection fantasies expressed in art and literature have been interpreted psychoanalytically as vehicles to express the ideas of perpetual erection and sensuality after death, reunion with a lost object, and attempts to deal with castration anxiety. They have also been interpreted along lines of generativity, including wishes for oral-incorporation and parthenogenesis, which achieve expression through efforts to perpetuate the connection with lost objects by taking them into the self in order to assure the other's and one's own immortality. Most interpretations combine and condense variations on several of those themes. Further, most attempts to interpret resurrection themes in art psychoanalytically do not contradict the various nonpsychoanalytic interpretations.

Erection, the "Erection-Resurrection Equation," and Perpetual Erection

The evidence from art and theology that Steinberg marshals for his erection-resurrection equation suggests a uniperspectival approach in interpreting the erection symbolism. In what appears to be an outright rejection of a psychoanalytic approach to the interpretation of these images, Steinberg offers instead a wholly theological-historical interpretation. In his view, it is the incarnation of Christ that accounts for the juxtaposition of penile erection images with visual depictions of Christ's resurrection. He downplays any contribution that sexual fantasy, particularly the wish for sustained erotic pleasure after death, may make to guiding a more psychoanalytically based interpretation. Yet to document his theological thesis, he tantalizingly presents an analysis of the erection-resurrection juxtaposition that would tempt any psychoanalytically inclined interpreter to add the sexual-erotic perspective to the simple incarnational view.

Steinberg cites Boccaccio's famous tenth tale of the third day, in which Alibech, in her attempt to do holy deeds, is seduced by Rustico, who convinces her that the act of intercourse is the means to her salvation. "And his [Rustico's] longings blazed more fiercely than ever, bringing about the resurrection of the flesh. Alibech stared at this in amazement and said: 'Rustico, what is that thing I see sticking out in front of you, which I do not possess?' " (Boccaccio 1350b, 316). Boccaccio, through Rustico's voice in offering a religious explanation for his propositioning, concludes with the moral,

> "And so, young ladies, if you stand in need of God's grace, see that you learn to put the devil back in Hell, for it is really to his liking and pleasurable to the parties concerned, and a great deal of good can *arise* [emphasis mine] and flow in the process." (319)

Steinberg thus finds the "locus classicus" in Western literature for the erection-resurrection equation to be this tenth tale of the third day in *The Decameron*. He believes, paradoxically, that the blasphemous irony in announcing the anchorite Rustico's sexual arousal, "la resurrezion della carne"—the resurrection of the flesh following its mortification—is an apt and effective pun removing the vulgarly sexual from the context of the novella. However, the 1930 Random House edition of *The Decameron* (Boccaccio 1350a) states merely "then his flesh grew stiff," dropping the pun and the blasphemy to preserve only the lewd, according to Steinberg.

D. H. Lawrence, in his 1928 short story "The Man Who Died," an allegorical tale of Christ's resurrection, makes a similarly humorous attempt to vulgarize what was later to be the erection-resurrection equation. In this fictionalized account of the Passion, Christ knows with certainty that he has risen from the dead only when he feels sexual stirrings and the overpowering desire for corporeal sexual merger with a woman. In marked distinction to Steinberg, who insisted on a purely theological meaning of the erection-resurrection equation, Lawrence's work is peppered with bawdy, vulgar, and in no way sacred imagery. For example, as the man who stands for Christ is risen, he carries a cock, a bird which "gleams with bright aloneness, though he answers the lure of hens" (418). To continue the vulgar, in contrast to what Steinberg regarded as Boccaccio's finesse and sublimated wit, Lawrence writes, "the cock of the man who had died sprang forth" and the man said, "Thou at least hast found thy kingdom, and the females to thy body. Thy aloneness can take on splendour, polished by the lure of thy hens" (420). At a date following his resurrection, he meets in Egypt a woman in search of the dead-but-returned-to-life god Osiris, to satisfy the sexual desires of the goddess Isis whom she serves. The woman mistakes the dead Christ for Osiris and follows through on her mission to rouse him to life sexually so that he can penetrate her mistress. Lawrence's Christ, who had initially accepted the "noli me tangere which separates the reborn from the vulgar" (431), felt, upon being taken for Osiris, stirrings in his loins, and allowed the wounds of the Passion to be anointed by the sensuous touch of the woman in sexual search: "I have risen naked and branded" (439). His death meant nothing as "he crouched to her, and he felt the blaze of his manhood rise up in his loins, magnificent. 'I am risen'" (444). The woman then cries, "I am full of the dead Osiris." The man who had died laughed to himself: "I have sowed the seed of my life and my resurrection, and put my touch forever upon the choice woman of this day" (449).

As further documentation for his theologically based equation, ever insistent that it contains nothing like Lawrence's vulgarity, Steinberg refers to Sebastiano Piombo's *Raising of Lazarus,* in which the loincloth of the resurrected Lazarus, like that in many paintings of Christ's resurrection, "dips unsupported between the thighs, firmly propped from below—a sign of resurgent flesh" (1983, 90). In a footnote he adds, "But we are now posing a novel question: whether in a picture of 1520, the sexual member could participate in resurrection symbolism. And we are shown a positive answer when we follow the roll of the loincloth from thigh to thigh" (90). In asking whether the erection-resurrection equation in paintings of circa 1530 is admissible in Christian ethos, Steinberg says a positive answer no longer seems scurrilous. He then develops his rationale of incarnation deriving strictly from Christian theology and legend to support his metaphoric equation. Two paintings by Maerten von Heemskerck (1525, 1532) of the *Man of Sorrows* show Christ resurrected and contain what Steinberg refers to as Heemskerck's outrageous conception of the Man of Sorrows, which, he says, has attempted a theologically based metaphor of the mortified, vivified flesh. Figures 10 and 11 show the fascinating contrast between Annibale Carracci's 1606 image of the dead Christ, with no visible erection, and Heemskerck's image of the resurrected Christ, displaying an obvious erection. Both paintings seen together do indeed appear to validate the erection-resurrection equation. Steinberg presented his interpretive rationale of the equation in Christian incarnational terms alone:

> He could have said or thought, something like this: if it was in the organ of generation and lust that Christ initiated his Passion; and if, in the exegetic tradition its circumcision on the eighth day prefigures the Resurrection, the final putting away of corruption; then what is that organ's status in the risen body? Or more simply: if the truth of the Incarnation was proved in the mortification of the penis, would not the truth of the Anastasis, the resuscitation, be proved by its erection? Would not this be the body's best show of power? (1983, 91)

Steinberg referred also to the glass painter who adapted Heemskerck's canvas to another resurrection scene and who had Christ in the copy appearing to rise from the tomb, as does the horned bull inserted between Christ's mounting thighs under his member.

Steinberg argues that images of erection in these visions of the resurrection are intended to prove the resuscitation of the flesh and are free of phallic sexual psychological meaning. Referring to a 1450 Van Weyden crucifixion scene, Steinberg says we have an acceptable

Figure 10. Before the resurrection, the flesh is dead. (Annibale Carracci, *Dead Christ* [1606]. Staatsgalerie, Stuttgart.)

Figure 11. After the resurrection of the flesh, the "erection-resurrection equation" is abundantly clear. (Maerten von Heemskerck, *Man of Sorrows* [1532]. Museum voor Schone Kunsten, Ghent.)

circumvention of the prohibited member—a potent synecdoche "that celebrates the thing covered in the magnificence bestowed on that covering: I mean the enhanced loincloth of Christ on the Cross" (91). These loincloths are often furled into flying banners, buoyed up by an indwelling breeze where all else is becalmed: "Only the inherent metaphoricity of Renaissance realism could exalt the humblest of garments to such efflorescence, and convert the *ostentatio genitalium* decently into a fanfare of cosmic triumph" (91).

Steinberg's limiting of his interpretational options to Christian incarnational theology would highlight the normative or communally based ideological common ground as a basis for interpretation. Adding the psychoanalytic perspective makes room for the more idiosyncratic interpretations—the perverse, the pathological psychological meanings attributable to the phallic fanfare of cosmic triumph.

A more psychological way of interpreting the juxtaposition of resurrection and erection imagery must account for something in the Northern Renaissance paintings of Heemskerck that Steinberg did not address, and that is the prominent display of the crown of thorns. In addition to its religious symbolism as part of the flagellation and the crucifixion paraphernalia, the image carries some surplus meaning, mainly having to do with masochism. Kaplan's characterization of Emma Bovary's perverse sexual submission and her attraction to Jesus' sufferings on the cross does deal with the psychological underpinnings of submission in imagery of whips, thorns, and flagellation. Many pictorial renderings of the crown of thorns are also reminiscent of the many themes and variations of "the red rose and the green briar" motif, which is symbolic of the Liebestod fantasy. Here is an instance where motifs of erection and of reunion with a lost object are condensed in one particular symbol of resurrection. Steinberg, himself, does not appear to pay much attention to possible interpretations of merger and reunion in resurrection imagery but only to erection.

There is obviously something vulgar about juxtaposing the sacred and the profane in the erection-resurrection equation. Tillich, in a personal communication to Lifton (1979), contrasted the vulgar theology of resurrection and afterlife imagery usually reserved for the "common people" with the more transformed symbolic theologies denoting spiritual attainment. As I shall subsequently illustrate, my patient's enactments of resurrection fantasies were indeed vulgar, and of course Boccaccio's connection of erection with "la resurrezion della carne" captures a quintessential vulgarization that would appeal to ignorant people and sophisticates alike. These kinds of analogies with resurrection are, according to Steinberg, too banal and blasphemous for plain iteration, as he has attempted in his erection-resurrection equation. The idea of blasphemy is important in various ways. In nonreligious spheres, it may take the form of desecration, defamation, and illicitness in regard to respected values surrounding death and burial. In psychopathological conditions, blasphemy is frequently encountered in the scenarios of sexual perversion. Religious blasphemy may be, among other things, a vicissitude of these urges.

Reunion with Lost Objects

The oral aspects of reunion, merger, and immortality fantasies that touch on the wish for rejoining the dead, for reunion and merger with a lost object, have received significant attention among psychoanalysts. Lewin (1950) in his work on the oral triad maintained that wishes/fears to sleep, to be devoured, and to eat, even to devour corpses, contain death wishes that mask the belief in the possibility of ultimate reunion in an immortal symbiosis. He believed these fantasies precede or supersede fears of dying which are castration equivalents or punishments for oedipal transgressions. Similarly, Pollock (1975) traces the origin of the concept of heaven to a universal fantasy of regressive symbiotic reunion with the archaic mother, a merger state that serves as a defense against object loss. Those fantasies of oral incorporation relate more to resurrection of lost objects than they do to more narcissistic self-resurrection fantasies that do not necessarily include fusion and merger with the object who is now dead.

The important theme of Christ's resurrection and bodily ascension to join his father in heaven is elaborated particularly in the resurrection sculptures of Michelangelo, which suggest Christ's longing for reunion with the father, or, in psychoanalytic terms, his negative oedipal wishes. The artist's attraction to this particular subject matter is a natural outgrowth, according to Liebert (1983), of Michelangelo's homosexual orientation. Psychoanalysis is familiar with the equation of death with reunion and might even identify a resurrection mythology embodying fantasies of reunion or merger, upon dying, with lost objects of childhood: the preoedipal mother, or the father of the negative oedipal phase who may be fused with the preoedipal mother, or even the oedipal parent of the opposite sex. Liebert's pathographic study of Michelangelo's life and images convincingly marshals evidence not just for the artist's unconscious conflicts that motivated his choice of subject matter and its depiction but also for his reliance on the forms and traditions of antiquity. Michelangelo's work contains elements of a particular form of reunion fantasy and indicates a "body-phallus equation" (Lewin 1946; see figure 12 in this volume), which may here be regarded as a version of the erection-resurrection equation. Liebert concludes,

> The dialectic between the concern with the destruction of the body and the restoration of it in idealized form operates throughout Michelangelo's art. . . . It is suggested by Michelangelo's many drawings of the Resurrection of Christ, in which Christ, represented like some beautiful Greek athlete, effortlessly steps out of his sarcophagus or soars upward in his conquest over death to a union with the Almighty Father. Perhaps the most telling example of the artistic resolution of this internal conflict is the statue of the *Dying Slave*. (1983, 116)

Liebert's interpretation suggests condensation of a fantasy of reunion with a preoedipal mother along with one of reunion with the father of the negative oedipal phase. It also suggests Michelangelo's yearning for only the negative oedipal object; that is, it expresses a wish for union and reunion with the idealized father imago, which, in this instance, was related to homosexual wishes. Lifton, in a similar vein, says that penis envy "may well be related to female envy of immortalizing male power" (1979, 33). Though originally phallic,

Figure 12. Far from the traditional iconographic representation, Christ "like some beautiful Greek athlete effortlessly steps out of his sarcophagus and soars upward." (Michelangelo, *Resurrection of Christ*, drawing [1532]. Louvre. Giraudon/Art Resource, New York.)

the organ later, says Lifton, can be equated with the ultimate symbolization of life continuity, as around work and works. This theme of generativity overlaps with the erection-resurrection equation, but holds meaning beyond it as well.

At this juncture, it is most appropriate to introduce a particular reunion-resurrection theme in the context of resurrection fantasies in women. Mostly, people tend to think of men rather than women as craving immortality. The major figure we think of in connection with resurrection is Christ. The reunion of Christ with the father lends itself to many psychoanalytic interpretations regarding the underlying psychology of reunion fantasies in men with all their preoedipal, positive oedipal, and negative oedipal implications. But what about resurrection fantasies involving women? Far less attention has been paid to the resurrection of Mary, referred to in the Christian creed as the Assumption of the Virgin. Although Mary's rise to heaven is celebrated widely on the Feast day of August 15, her actual death is rarely mentioned, in contrast to that of her son. She is, however, as Marina Warner (1976) tells us in her feminist treatise on the myth and the cult of the Virgin Mary, "taken up to heaven, to lie there in her glorified body, as a promise of the resurrection of the flesh that will come to every creature." It was only in a 1950 Papal Bull that there was any definitive recognition of the Catholic dogma of the Assumption of the Virgin:

> When Pope Pius XII appeared on the balcony of St. Peter's on November 1, 1950, to address a crowd of nearly a million strong, his announcement that "Mary was taken up body and soul into the glory of heaven" was greeted with thunderous clapping, with tears of joy and resonant prayers. It was the climax of centuries of tradition, and the delay had been caused only by the absence of scriptural sources. But the Vatican sources invoking the holy spirit had returned to their books, and the problem had been overcome. *The Assumption dogma had depended on the Christian equivalence between sex and death and consequently between the Virgin's purity and her freedom from the dissolution of the grave.* (Warner 1976, 92 [italics mine])

Unlike her son, whose body is entombed and who wrestles in limbo with the forces of death, and then rises, Mary is spared the throes of death. Her body is reanimated immediately after death with no dormition, no period suggestive of falling asleep. Her resurrection often appears as an aside. Warner's point is that the focus on the flesh, in the case of Mary, is far less than that of her son. She is not fully humanized, as he is, but is simply idealized. Her rise is no more important than that of any mortal on Judgment Day.

Peter told Jesus, "thou shouldst raise the body of thy mother and take her with thee rejoicing to heaven." This reunion story demands an interpretation of the joining of Christ after his Ascension with his mother Mary, after her Assumption, as more than a simple preoedipal merger of virginal mother and asexual child. Oedipal overtones cannot be dismissed. In quite a few pictorial representations, Mary is depicted as the Bride of Christ and the Queen of Heaven. In the twelfth-century mosaic located in the church of Santa Maria in Trastevere in Rome, this imagery, according to Warner, becomes explicit, as Mary is triumphantly assumed into heaven and embraced by Christ: "Her youthful beauty, unquestionably accepted from that day on, has a theological purpose: the Virgin is no longer dowager queen mother, but the beloved Shulamite, bride of Christ" (Warner 1976, 22). Another chaste depiction of the adored nuptial couple is to be found in the medieval illustration by Jean Colombe (see figure 13). According to Warner, the love songs of Solomon and the Shulamite in the Song of Songs were predominantly applied to the love between Christ and the consecrated Virgin: "it still remains astonishing that an ascetic religion should ever have included in its sacred canon a text so remarkable for its undisguised sexuality." Warner, like Steinberg, presents an analysis of sexual imagery, focusing on the erotic as well as the tender feelings in Mary. Warner singles out the popular fourteenth-century legend, frequently depicted in the art of the Renaissance, in which the Virgin lets her sash or girdle fall to earth at the time of her assumption in order to convince doubting Thomas of her ascent, a clearly symbolic act: "The sexuality of the symbol derives from its tantalizing ambivalence: loosed, the girdle gives promise: fastened, it denies. In that sense it is a mirror image of the virgin bride" (Warner 1976, 279). Interestingly, Christians pray over the relics of the Virgin's girdle that the curse of infidelity be lifted from them.

Figure 13. The Virgin Mary is taken up, in her glorified body, as her son's Queen of Heaven, a promise of resurrection of the flesh that will come to every living creature. (Jean Colombe, *The Celestial Court* [Coronation of the Virgin, 1345]. Musée Condé, Chantilly. Giraudon/Art Resource, New York.)

While Warner documents the Virgin as her son's bride in Heaven, Binion (1993) daringly develops the idea that the prostitute, Mary Magdalene, was "by tradition the betrothed of Christ, their nuptials to be celebrated on high. Perhaps this is why she enjoyed the unique iconological practice of ascending to heaven stark naked" (76). Binion was referring to a 1501 Lucas Cranach woodcut and a 1504 Dürer etching, among other works. Like the sexuality of Christ in Renaissance art, documented by Steinberg, the iconological depiction of the voluptuous nude burning with love for Christ and his resurrected flesh faded into oblivion in latter day artistic renditions and by the nineteenth century, the Magdalene was simply a figure of "carnality postponed" (Binion 1993, 85). As we have already noted, however, D. H. Lawrence (1928) revived the image of burning passion of the flesh between the resurrected Christ and the resurrected Magdalene in his short story. The "noli me tangere" was indeed transformed. Steinberg's thesis that Christ's sexuality was merely a theological metaphor for incarnation seems dubiously valid in the face of these various early and later interpretations; Binion's conclusions are more persuasive and certainly more consistent with a psychoanalytic point of view.

Another well known image in Christian tradition of death and divine love is expressed in the autobiography of Saint Teresa of Avila, in which she told how she tasted the great love of God:

> An angel in bodily form, such as I am not in the habit of seeing except very rarely . . . not tall, but short, and very beautiful. . . . In his hands I saw a great golden spear, and at the iron tip there appeared to be a point of fire. This he plunged into my heart several times so that it penetrated to my entrails. When he pulled it out, I felt that he took them with it, and left me utterly consumed by the great love of God. The pain was so severe that it made me utter several moans. The sweetness caused by this intense pain is so extreme that one cannot possibly wish it to cease, nor is one's soul content then with anything but God. (Cohen 1957, 210)

Nothing better conveys the obvious sexual love masquerading behind the facade of divine love than Bernini's sculpture, *Saint Theresa in Ecstasy,* found in the Coronaro Chapel of the church of S. Maria della Vittoria in Rome (see figure 14). In this representation, Theresa falls back in a swoon, lips parted, foot hanging bare below the hem of her full robes. As sexual as this divine love may appear to the psychoanalytically informed, it does not diminish the spiritual reality of the experience for Catholics, or its theological impact. Bernini's work contains a perfect example lending itself to the interface of psychoanalytic interpretation (of repressed sexuality in a Liebestod) and theological interpretation (the vision as a mediating instrument between heaven and earth).

Both Mary and St. Teresa provide examples of supernatural qualities coexisting within a human body that is real. Mary's physical reality in her Assumption and the proof of her corporeality by the girdle, or sash dropped to doubting Thomas is as important to her devotees as was the incarnated resurrected body of Christ. That assumed body, however, was disputed by those non-Catholic churches that disliked the glory paid equally to mother and son, to woman and man.

Decay, Purification, and Exhuming

In the Catholic cult of the Virgin, Mary's body smells ambrosial. Warner reminds us that lilies or roses spring up in her empty tomb in paintings of the Assumption, as in Pinturicchio's mille-fleurs evocation in the Borgia apartments of the Vatican, and in the French fleur-de-lis symbol. The stench of death and bodily decomposition, however, describe evil. Putrefaction, in Catholic doctrine, is the God-given penalty of the Fall. On Ash Wednesday, priests remind parishioners, "Remember, man, dust thou art and to dust thou shalt return." Mary, the lily of the field, the Rose of Sharon, is spared the putrefaction that mortal bodies suffer. Decay and purification are themes of the resurrection with a clearly sexual connotation, extending into the fantasy life of many, and to be illustrated in my case presentation of Dr. D. Warner conveys the close connection between putrefaction of the dead body and ideas that sexual union also destroys the body, in the sense of the merger feelings in the blurred body contours during ecstatic, orgastic experiences:

Figure 14. Nothing better conveys the obvious sexual love masquerading behind the facade of divine love. (Gian Lorenzo Bernini, *Saint Theresa in Ecstasy* [1645–52]. S. Maria della Vittoria, Rome.)

This is what Augustine may have feared when he inveighed the vileness of lust: the loss of control of self, the *petit mort,* as the French call orgasm. The operations of lust and of death on the body are kinsmen in Christian symbolism; and the puns it works on are almost cutely witty. (1976, 98)

Christian resurrection mythology has among its most important functions the overcoming of dread about the decay and dissolution of the body. Rising from the grave to an eternal life, enfleshed, signifies purification. Reunion of the pure soul with the intact body, not the one that has crumbled to dust, is a theme transcending the bounds of Christianity, is to be found in the lives of many individuals, and holds a particularly prominent place in the fantasy life of the patient who will be described in the next chapter.

In the life of Mary, this theme is particularly prominent, as she was never entombed, never fated to suffer any death or decay, any corruption of the flesh in life or dissolution of the body at her life's termination. Christ simply raises her up and takes her joyously into heaven to rejoin him. Unlike the sinful Adam, Mary and Jesus did not dissolve into dust. Dust and dirt are easily associated with impurity, just as sexuality is. As Mary was pure and asexual in life, so does her Assumption without any time spent decaying in a coffin stand for sexual purity at death. Agelessness and immortality are hers because her purity guarantees freedom from corruption and time, whereas decay marks the passage of years.

Resurrection: Shame, Guilt, and Conflict

Scenes depicting both the resurrection of the dead and the resurrection of Christ bring to life the possibility of human nature without guilt or shame:

The resurrected, both male and female, shall not be ashamed in heaven . . . St. Thomas writes "though there be difference of sex, there will be not shame in seeing one another, since there will be no lust to invite them to shameful deeds which are the cause of shame." (Steinberg 1983, 20)

This conflict-free state achieves its graphic representation mainly in the nudity of the resurrected human beings. Renaissance images frequently depict the dead Christ and the resurrected Christ as nude and frankly sensual. Nudity, then, would appear frequently to represent longings for a paradise where there is no shame, no guilt, *no burdens of conflict.* Steinberg believes that Michelangelo's sculpture is particularly expressive of these wishes:

> If Michelangelo denuded his *Risen Christ,* he must have sensed a rightness in his decision more compelling than inhibitions of modesty; must have seen that a loincloth would convict those genitalia of being "pudenda," therefore denying the very work of redemption which promised to free nature from its Adamic contagion of shame. (18–20)

Pudenda, from the Latin *pudendere,* "to be ashamed," refers to genitalia with the connotation of shame. Steinberg attributes to the nudity in representations of Christ, particularly the genital exposure, even more importance than the nudity of ordinary individuals. Such unabashed freedom in Christian teaching was, he said, reserved only for Christ and for those who would resurrect in Christ's likeness. Steinberg argues that Michelangelo's rendition of the *Risen Christ* is nude in order to express the theological idea that Christ must be exempt from genital shame. Steinberg puzzles that some Michelangelo scholars see the historical roots of the statue's undress outside of Christianity and embedded only in the context of antiquity from which it derives (see Liebert 1983). He argues that it is not pagan nudism that inspired images of Christ nude, but that the iconography derives from Christian content itself, expressing the competing claims of mortality and the exemptive nature of Christ's body.

A psychoanalytic reading of those same images must consider that resurrection fantasies which express the wish for perpetual erection and nondying sensuality also express a wish for a conflict-free state transcending the guilt and shame inherent in both positive and negative oedipal situations. To buttress his argument that the exposed genitalia are meant to convey the theological justification of the time for Christ's purity and absence of guilt or shame, Steinberg treats extensively certain particular Renaissance images of the dead Christ in which the father is gazing at or touching the nude son's genitals:

> But what makes the images I am citing rare and psychologically trou-
> bling is the Father's intrusive gesture, his unprecedented acknowledg-
> ment of the Son's loins. Nothing in received iconography sanctions it;
> and common intuition proscribes it . . . the natural distance and shame
> shown between father and sons caves in before our eyes—wherein
> the divine Father's only-begotten . . . is a virgin, virginally conceived,
> enfleshed, sexed, circumcised, sacrificed and so restored to the Throne
> of Grace. (1983, 107–8)

According to Steinberg, the Northern Renaissance images of the painfully intimate metaphor of the father's hand on the groin of the son, which breached a universal taboo was also, paradoxically, the fittest symbol of divine reconcilement. No art images in subsequent times contained this metaphor, but the latter incomprehension and oblivion is profound. Steinberg claims it is the price paid by the modern world for its massive historic retreat from the mythical grounds of Christianity.

Psychoanalytic readings must also consider the ways in which these images depict a condensation of a wish for a guilt-free state vis-à-vis the oedipal father with a wish for homosexual or negative or even preoedipal merger. There is room for a multiperspectival interpretation of nudity in the representations of Christ and of the father's involvement with the son's nudity that goes far beyond Steinberg's time-bound nonpsychological, Christian iconographical reading of the incarnation. The ideas inspiring these images are rooted both in antiquity and in the Christian iconographical tradi-tions of representing incarnation. The roots, however, go beyond both of these historical, time-bound sources. The looking and touch-ing also reflect timeless psychological longings (see figure 15) such as the universal wish to be free of conflict when it comes to expressing oedipal longings, or negative oedipal-homosexual longings, as well as preoedipal yearnings for blissful reunion with either the father or with a genderless figure of the preoedipal phase.

Figure 15. Looking and touching among the resurrected dead reflect timeless psychological longings and not simply the humanation and incarnation
of Christ. (Victor-Louis Mottez, *The Resurrection of the Dead* [1896].
Musée de Beaux Arts, Lille. Giraudon/Art Resource, New York.)

Circumcision, Castration, and Resurrection

Since corpses do not move their hands in a way so as to touch the groin, and fathers do not touch the groins of their dead sons, as they do in motifs found in so many of the lamentations, entombments, and Pietàs, Steinberg argues that these motifs must point back to what he considers their origin, that is, to the circumcision of Christ. He sees the dead Christ touching his groin in the completed Passion as a pointing back to the beginning, as the blood in the "blood-hyphen" runs from the last wound back to the first. Whether or not the artists consciously or unconsciously had in mind this connection of the first wound of the circumcision with the last wound of the Passion, Steinberg's position that the circumcision on the eighth day prefigures the resurrection could not have evolved without some underlying acknowledgment of castration symbolism contributing to this particular interpretation of the significance of the blood-hyphen. To make the connection, Steinberg invokes certain Biblical interpretations of numbers. One such states that the number seven, signifying rest, is proper to the souls who rest in anticipation of the glory of the resurrection. The number eight, which signifies beatitude, fits those who having already received back their bodies, rejoicing in blessed immortality. He understands the circumcision on the eighth day of life as prefiguring Christ's resurrection on the eighth day of the Passion. Eight stands for renewal and regeneration and the circumcision, he says, authenticates the incarnation, launches the Passion, and prefigures the resurrection. All of this numerology is very interesting in light of the debate among theologians as to whether the resurrected Christ was in a body still circumcised—Jewish—as he was born—or with the foreskin restored, Christian, following events of the Passion. Whatever the outcome of this debate, Steinberg's thesis of continuity between commencement and consummation is symbolized by the blood-hyphen as it extends from breast wound to groin. The blood of the Passion, culminating on the cross in the blood of the sacred heart, was foretold by the blood that begins in the penis of the circumcision. There actually were sermons in the fifteenth century, according to John O'Malley, Steinberg's discussant, substantiating this position. The sermons dealt with the notion that the first wound and the first shedding of blood in the Passion both contain signs of Christ's genuine humanity in the service of redemption.

∽

At this point in my presentation, I have reviewed the relevant background and elaborated most of the major psychoanalytic interpretations of resurrection imagery in art and in the individual psyche. I will now present a summary of some case material of a patient whose resurrection fantasies were central to his analysis. In exploring this man's fantasies and their enactments, I was able to find clear parallels between the symbolic meaning of his fantasies and symptoms and the various underlying meanings in the art that I have been discussing. His mental life seems to span the gamut of categories that I have been focusing on in art: the erection-resurrection equation; reunion and merger; self-perpetuation via immortality; castration, guilt, and shame; parthenogenesis and oral incorporation; and decay and purification. In presenting my material, I shall be making discursions back and forth between the material presented in this chapter dealing with psychoanalytic interpretations as applied to resurrection themes in art and life, and the clinical interpretations of a patient in psychoanalytic therapy. In this attempt to integrate resurrection motifs in art with resurrection fantasies in life, I shall always be thinking of the normative and pathological aspects of love and death.

Six

Resurrection Themes in Life: A Case Study

$\mathcal{D}$r. D was a surgeon who had engaged in a lifelong pattern of passionate, compulsively driven, extramarital, "dangerous" sexual liaisons with women he regarded as "femmes fatales." In his later years, this pattern was overwhelming him with symptomatic anxieties. He entered treatment with me in his sixties because of a tormenting inability to extricate himself from a painful relationship with a woman who had fallen in love with him, as he had with her. Her relentless pursuit of him bore uncanny similarities to the portrayal by Glenn Close of the seemingly surreal "vampire" lady in the film *Fatal Attraction*. She pursued not only him, but me as his analyst as well, harassing both of us with suicide threats, letters, phone calls, message taping, and persistent "hang-up" calls in her driven efforts to verify his whereabouts. She pleaded with me to let her join him in sessions and tried to intimidate me into persuading him to leave his wife because she had proof he loved her more. The patient, who was "hopelessly" in love, felt helpless to deal with these pressures and tactics. He felt unable, by and large, to resist his own underlying temptations to submit to the potentially "fatal" but sexually exciting pulls of their liaison. His symptomatic chronic panic states over his lack of control in the face of her seductiveness became the focus of the treatment.

These severe anxieties took the form, manifestly, of a fear of being caught and of death. It soon became apparent that he hoped to ward off his own death in a number of mostly superstitious ways. In seeking out "illicit" forms of intercourse with certain perverse aims, Dr. D lived out fantasies of being masochistically beaten, flagellated, and particularly of "dying in the saddle" with the femme fatale to whom he felt attracted. In his imagination, these events were spectacles witnessed by others and remembered eternally. Yet, he superstitiously warded off death in a wide variety of symbolic ways. In tending to his garden, he hoped to exhume from the soil his vision of recurrent blooms and eternal life. By sleeping in an upright position, he hoped to ward off death, which he feared would be prematurely visited upon him should he succumb to the yielding sleep of the prone position. In restoring old junk to become original and new beautiful objects, he enacted a wish to revitalize inanimate, decayed, and decaying substances to life and perpetuity. He would retrieve old castaways from the gutters of the rich: a sled, a flowerpot, a toilet bowl chain from which he forged a modern abstract sculpture, and restore them to a new form, resurrecting them from the trashed-out dead. He pursued his sexual escapades, his work, and his avocations of gardening, art appreciation, and restoration of discarded objects with a drivenness that betrayed overriding wishes to leave his mark and memories, to resurrect himself so that others would remember him, as outstanding in all of these spheres. Dr. D was a "would-be-artist," warding off his fear of the "bad death" through the pursuit of illicit and what he fantasized as eternal sexuality, as well as through his avocational art pursuits, both of which he enacted compulsively to grant him a new lease on life. Yet, the more he feared the "bad death," the more inextricably bound he became to his femme fatale, and the more bound to her, the more terrified he became of submitting to his masochism, a pattern that could be read as a male version of the *Hörigkeit* scenario.

Dr. D's concerns about death appeared to surface only late in life, in connection with the deadly consequences he anticipated in response to his uncontrolled sexual indiscretions. He also had to contend with a mild cardiac condition and other medical problems which undoubtedly are not rare among the elderly or aging patient in analytic therapy. However, Dr. D's worries actually started in childhood and by the age of seventeen they had become an obsessive preoccupation. At that time, he entertained morbid thoughts about his grandparents' visible signs of bodily deterioration. However, we must not confound these existential, conscious preoccupations with their dynamically unconscious motivations, for he remembered those adolescent years as a time of severe beatings by his father for what sounds to be age-appropriate sexual experimentation. Memories of decomposition of the flesh thus were condensed with masochistically gratifying fantasies of being beaten for forbidden sexual forays.

Dr. D's obsession with his femme fatale stimulated him to attempt to realize his fantasies of immortality. As he would tell me of his illicit sexuality, an erotic transference developed as he drew me into his circle of fatal attractions. He languished in fantasies of seducing me, of sinning lasciviously and carrying through these activities in Purgatory, where he would have liked to stay indefinitely. God's punishments were, he said, the price he paid in his bargain with the devil to continue his earthly delights in whatever locale he would occupy in the afterlife.

With advancing age, illness, diminution of potency, and accumulating social slights in response to his uncontrolled exhibitionistic sexual indiscretions, and, not incidentally, in his transferential feelings toward me, Dr. D chose to shift to relative abstinence as a new way of life. He began to identify with the martyred Christ in many ways. Resurrection fantasies became more apparent and driving forces than they were at the start of his analysis, when he was hardly abstinent but very active sexually in his dangerous liaisons. When he felt forced by age, illness, and feared social slights to limit his extramarital sexual activity, Dr. D thought he knew chastity as Christ did, and this belief fostered his Christ identification and the accompanying resurrection fantasies, which contained elements of both the resurrection of Christ and the Last Judgment.

It became clear in the course of the analysis that Dr. D's resurrection fantasies, like the images of resurrection in Renaissance art, condensed a multiplicity of unconscious fantasies. Prominent among them was a wish to recreate himself, parthenogenetically, through his idiosyncratic oeuvre. The oeuvre of this "would-be-artist" consisted, for one, of his fantasy of the legacy he would leave to the next-generation doctor, whom he fantasized as his replacement and who would inspect and admire the reconstructive work that he had performed on his former patients. The man who would continue Dr. D's practice would view Dr. D's unsurpassed, perfect record of exquisite surgical incisions and restorations, praising his work and promoting his immortality. It also consisted of some very concrete representations of all the art knowledge that he had accumulated and had "poured into his head," which he would then pour into the heads of his children, grandchildren, and anyone who wished to read his autobiography, which he was dreaming of writing for them. His oeuvre extended to his select collection of antiquities and primitive art, to his perfectly crafted carvings, all of which he kept polished and shiny in anticipation of their becoming part of his estate. Additionally, he had a collection of old discarded literal junk, which he had restored by rubbing down and bringing out the original finishes, for posterity to admire. As much as anything else, his oeuvre consisted of his memory traces of all the world's greatest art that he liked to imagine that he had created, himself. In fanciful moments, he imagined that a brain autopsy could preserve his mental acquisitions forever. His oeuvre was epitomized by his ever-renewable garden, of which more shall be said shortly.

Dr. D had been told by friends that he can be quite crude and offensive to women, that he defiled them through excessive "womanizing." One is reminded of a passage in Lifton's (1979) book, where Norman Mailer is quoted. Mailer is quite explicit about the male quest for immortality via the encounter with the female and her "seat of creation." This quest, Mailer says, is a cause for such a man to detest women, to "defile them, humiliate them, defecate symbolically upon them, do everything to reduce them so that one might dare to enter them and take pleasure of them" (Lifton 1979,

32, citing Mailer 1971). In this reference to man's envy of women, Lifton says that the envy of which Mailer speaks is a life-creating envy, an immortality envy. Out of that envy man degrades woman, for she is seen as the source, possessor, and guardian of the life process itself, "and of the sexual union as an absolute expression of centering in which the immediate blends with the ultimate and the present with a sense of timelessness" (33). Dr. D's fear/wish of "dying in the saddle" related in this way to his degradation of the women he got close to.

It became clear in the course of his analysis that Dr. D's resurrection fantasies, like the images of Christ's resurrection in Renaissance art, condensed a multiplicity of unconscious fantasies, all accompanying the proliferation of death anxieties which increased with age, illness, and curtailment of sexual activities. Prominent among them was a wish to achieve immortality and recreate himself in various ways that would force others to remember him. He memorized all he could of the world's great art, wishing he had created it himself. A favorite haunt for seducing women was a local art museum where his personal attractiveness, he believed, would be enhanced as women idealized his stored knowledge of immortal art and art immortals.

One particular preoccupation was expressed in his belief that only artists can be immortal: "I wish I could reinvent the safety pin, or something like it. That would be enough for me." That is, he would accept this variation of creative accomplishment as an adequate substitute for attaining the creative perfection of his lifelong ego ideal, who was Picasso. He chose Picasso because of the longevity in both the sexual and artistic spheres of his life. Our would-be-artist also admired art that carries messages of immortality and of the possibility of the afterlife. He always liked Thornton Wilder's *Our Town* (1938), a play that takes place in a graveyard, in which the protagonist meets all the people of her childhood who had predeceased her. In fact, Dr. D referred to this play in the eulogy he delivered at his father's funeral. He was also intensely interested in Florentine Renaissance artists. At the age of fourteen he had read Benvenuto Cellini's autobiography, and was so impressed with the miracles that the Italian craftsman had sculpted out of gold that one cannot help but wonder if Dr. D's choice of surgery, which involves intricate handiwork in "resculpting" body parts, was in part motivated by this early enchantment. In adolescence, he kept track of the lives of the Italian artists, the Medicis and Popes who were their patrons, and the donors who appear in the paintings they commissioned as a way of assuring their own immortality by resurrecting themselves in the memories of their viewers. The patronage system captured his imagination so that he seemed to have enacted a Renaissance-age drama in the terms of the cultural and economic condition of his own lifestyle. Adolescent fantasies about being sponsored by great men of power seem to have influenced his seeking and finding, as if this were the only sensible route to marriage, the equivalent of a patron in his father-in-law. Dr. D bought out the practice of an older doctor who promised to bequeath to Dr. D, once the younger man would replace the older, many wealthy and famous acquaintances as patients, most of whom were prominent in the worlds of the performing and creative arts. The murderous wishes stirred up in Dr. D, as his senior achieved unanticipated longevity and a long delay of the promised referrals, were later, and during analysis, projected onto his own potential replacements. His fear that they might wish to polish him off led to significant inhibitions in planning for his own eventual retirement.

Unconscious resurrection fantasies were also to be found in Dr. D's efforts to restore and preserve the body. The bones in particular, he was convinced, are immortal, for they alone are preserved over time in skeletal remains of the dead, just as he had preserved them in life. But Dr. D was not a mere preserver of the corpus. He regarded each and every surgical incision and reconstruction with the respect and devotion of an archaeologist who aims to preserve forever a relic from antiquity. He preserved, restored, and reconstructed with methodical care, patience, and pride. He explained to me, in accounting for his perfectionism (which in fact annoyed some of his patients and frightened away others), that if any of his deceased patients were to be autopsied, or their graves exhumed, the surgical reconstruction that was the object of his painstaking labors, the perfect artistic creation, would be immortalized in testimony to his professional perfection and scrupulous conscientiousness. These were the conscious fantasies. Unconsciously there was a web of others.

Dr. D fancied himself a true Renaissance man, though he knew he fell short. Like his boyhood idol, Cellini, he was more of a consummate craftsman than an imaginative artist. Our knowledge of his resurrection fantasies, together with our knowledge of some of his inner conflicts, helps to interpret the art he would aspire to create: the safety pin, the immortal phallic imagery of a Picasso, or the craftsmanship of the Florentine goldsmiths, each of whom had his patron and an apprentice to carry on the great tradition, assuring that any art to be judged as great through posterity would be the same now as, say, during the Sumerian era. As with a Wagner opera, we can identify leitmotifs in the life of this man. In this instance, they are resurrection subthemes that recur repetitively, and because of the drivenness of this man's preoccupations, we would categorize them as pathological despite their normative and universal roots.

Leitmotifs of Blasphemy, Exhuming, and Decay

Just as Steinberg's erection-resurrection equation might evoke in the minds of people of delicate sensibility protests of too much vulgarity, sacrilege, and blasphemy, so too might Dr. D's eccentric life style evoke a host of epithetic reactions.

Throughout his life, Dr. D displayed a pattern of behavior in which one might identify secular versions of religious defamation, profanation, sacrilege, and blasphemy. As a young man, he attempted to "purify" himself by changing his Jewish last name to one that sounded elegant and Christian to him and represented his counter-identification with aspects of his father's aggression and sexuality which he repudiated as being crude and vulgar. Yet, the vulgar infiltrated his everyday behavior in the form of symptoms. He regularly offended certain of his patients by invasive questioning when they were getting ready to go on the operating table, or when they could not talk; he degraded and defiled the women he made love with by treating them roughly and inconsiderately when they expected more tact and consideration than he was inclined to offer; he high-mindedly betrayed his trust as an officer and a gentleman in the army by taking on a fraudulent identity and illegally maneuvering a pleasure-trip to Paris in order to view great art and to visit some prostitutes during the height of the Nazi occupation. His trip to Paris for purposes of illicit sexual adventure was a conscious and deliberate attempt to achieve in reality what he had imagined in his adolescence to be the forbidden delights of a city which brought to life the lasciviousness he found in Lautrec's paintings of prostitutes. When he sought out the seedy and vulgar, however, it was usually in a context of wishing to defame the more sacred images he knew of in the many pictures of Paris that he had clipped and collected. The images that particularly impressed him in these secretly kept collections involved the juxtaposition of profane and sacred contents, suggesting to him the very vulgarity and crudeness that he repudiated in his father, but which gave him secret pleasures. On the illegal wartime trip, he headed straight for the neighborhood near the Church of Le Sacré Coeur where he photographed, with Le Sacré Coeur as backdrop, an artist with his nude model, thereby actualizing his boyhood thrill of thinking of Parisian whores as the only source of models for artists. He designated this photograph as part of his legacy, hoping it would be viewed by posterity as part of his "oeuvre." The would-be-artist hoped then to be associated in people's minds with the artists represented in his ego-ideal, such as Cellini or Picasso, whose privileged illicitness, when expressed in their eternally admired works, would guarantee immortality.

Idealizing of the vulgar, a leitmotif in the life of this would-be-artist, was always to be found in a context of both identifying with and defensively trying to undo and repudiate the strong unconscious identification with his father's vulgarity which he came to repudiate, consciously. Since childhood, he anticipated punishments, whippings, even arrest as a criminal for all of his own vulgarity. He masochistically wished to provoke reprimands, as in sessions. Often, he blew his nose vigorously, wiping it, putting the soaking tissues on a chair in my office where I and others sit. This apparent disregard of cleanliness and hygiene appears as a manifest contradiction of his meticulous cleanliness and quest for purification in his surgical practice.

This compulsive activity can be understood, then, as a repetitive enactment of certain scenes he had witnessed, and which irritatingly excited him, such as that of his vulgar father blowing his nose into a dinner napkin and then wiping his mouth with it. Dr. D did exactly that in his wife's presence. With me, in addition to the vigorous nose blowing, he "licked his chops" often as he told me of his illicit sexuality, his fantasies of seducing me, and his lifelong preoccupations with sinning lasciviously and of carrying through the activity in Purgatory, or limbo, where he hoped to stay indefinitely.

I regard his repetitive, compulsive "blasphemous" acts as reflecting a resurrection fantasy, especially as he changed his name from a Jewish to a Christian one, a change that unconsciously signified rebirth into a faith which held a belief in the afterlife, and where men, who were not circumcised as boys, need not live in shame. He had given a good deal of thought to the burial customs of different religions. He was troubled by the Jewish belief in the idea that bodies simply decomposed into dust following death, being more comfortable with the Christian ideas of purity in the possibility of resurrection. His fantasies contain the same sort of juxtaposed elements of vulgarity and divinity as appear prominently in the images of Christian theology selected by Steinberg from Renaissance art works to convey the sexuality of Christ and the erection-resurrection equation.

Related to blasphemy is Dr. D's preoccupation with decay and exhumation of dead substances. Juxtaposed with the lofty and glorious aspirations toward the aesthetic were a fascination with rotting, decayed, fecal, and necrotic substances and their symbolic equivalents. This juxtaposition has already been referred to in his perseverative, driven behavior in transforming junk into valuable restorations, and decaying skeletal supports into monuments of permanently resurrected bone, in testimony to his consummate skills as a surgeon and craftsman. His absorbing passion to dig deep into his patients' bodies to resurrect tissue and life might be characterized as variations on a theme of alchemy, or the wish to transform feces into gold, death into life. In Dr. D's personal fantasy life, in this variant of necromancy and perpetual revival, particular emphasis was directed to the place of hair, nails, urine, and feces. These substances, because they are infinitely renewable, lend themselves in conscious and unconscious fantasy as suitable material out of which one can forge an image of a self that can endure well into perpetuity. They thus can easily be appropriated to express resurrection ideas.

In his idealized body image, Dr. D made use of his own waste products in his wish to preserve his body as forever young, renewed, and never decayed and wasted. That is, his image of his glorious body suffused with a narcissistically enhancing self-feeling was not restricted to what have customarily been associated with the body as pure phallus. It extended beyond the phallic narcissistic imagery to accompany excreta as well. He relished the thought of spraying his urine throughout the world, imagining it evaporating and becoming part of the timeless cosmos. His feces could fertilize food supplies that others would ingest and then excrete, at which time they would generously transform into new food for new generations, and thus contribute to the chain of immortality. Dr. D continuously yearned for resurrection of his own precious bodily substances and this fantasy motivated a corpus of symptomatic compulsive behaviors which substantiated the notion that his resurrection fantasies incorporated pathological elements. He had indulged for years in certain compulsive toileting rituals of wiping himself spotlessly clean and flushing the toilet between each stool production of a given bowel movement, as though cleaning both the toilet bowl and his own anal orifice in an honoring manner, preparing them for a pristine state in which to receive the next produced stool. From time to time, he overblew his nose, belying a compulsion to rid it of all exudate. Although this compulsion to purify body orifices received sublimated outlet in his daily work of cleaning out wounds, antiseptically, he approached this task with perfectionistic zeal bordering on violence, which had threatened and alienated some of his patients.

His treatment of money, the nonorganic fecal equivalent, was, as would be expected, similar. Until his penuriousness was analyzed, he kept his holdings in a safe-deposit box where, although they earned no interest, he could touch and feel the cash as real, fearful of investing in a way that would inform him only on paper of accruals of his assets. Monthly statements from a broker, even those indicating growth of his assets, were not palpably real like growing piles of money that he could count and recount. An important aspect of his superstitious use of money and the collection of junk to be restored was their designation as inanimate, dead substances, like feces or mucus. He confessed to a (conscious) fear that the medical examiner at his death and at his autopsy would find the dirt, and that was one reason he offered for the compulsive cleaning and polishing of his own oral, aural, anal, nasal, and dermal orifices. Similarly, he explained that his perfectionism in performing antiseptic cleansing procedures on his patients was a way of assuring that they would go to their graves in a state of purification, and would therefore be a credit to his reputation should they ever be examined by the Department of Health. These purification rituals, then, were clearly related to some narcissistic aspects of immortality concerns. The purifying obsessions seem in large measure to be attempts to purify himself from the guilt of his indiscretions: "When I die, I don't want the doctor to see any dirt on me." All of these rituals illuminated his preoccupation with the revitalization of dead and inanimate substances, and reflected, along with the wish to be rid of guilt, his powerful resurrection wishes. The fantasy of his own resurrection in the form of a perfectly clean, polished, and repolished restoration of inanimate and decaying matter was acted out in countless ways. In one particularly fanciful version, he became obsessively preoccupied with discovering what restorative substance he imagined to be inside of a strange bottle kept by a collegial rival in his office. Although it looked to him to contain an ordinary solution, he was plagued by the possibility that it contained a secret elixir of life. That potion would enable his rival to prevent his own patients' bodies from ever decaying, while Dr. D, on the other hand, would have to risk the very shameful (to him) failures of an ordinary surgical practice. His patients would carry for all the world to see the evidence of their surgeon's falling short of professional perfection, which translated for Dr. D into the evidence of mortal decay. He fantasized that his own patients would, after his death, be examined by other surgeons, his successors, who would discover how he fell mortifyingly short of his fantasized accomplishments. (*Mortify:* to subdue or deaden, as the body or bodily passions, by abstinence or self-inflicted pain or discomfort; to become necrotic or gangrenous. How close the dictionary definition comes to, captures, this man's equation of shame with death and decay, underscores the existence of unconscious resurrection fantasies.)

These preoccupations accompanied memories referred to earlier, of his father and uncle vulgarly blowing their noses into their dinner napkins in public, suggesting an identification which he repudiated yet at the same time felt compelled to enact in my presence during the sessions. Interestingly, it was Dr. D's job as an army medical officer to "short-arm" the men, to pull back their penile foreskins, to detect excrescences that might be related to venereal disease. He also compulsively avoided or removed perspiration, and picked out all possible pimples and blackheads. Nothing was to be seen leaking from any orifice, even the tiniest pore. So he was constantly wiping his face, hands and neck. He often dwelled on the horror of the gas-chamber victims defecating and urinating and standing in their own excrement. These concerns were exacerbated when he involuntarily urinated during a mugging and also when he was interrogated by police for speeding, incidents he regarded as his closest brushes with death.

One reason that Dr. D was so fascinated by museums, and from a very young age, is that in them, the inanimate and the dead are preserved as immortal. He was constantly preoccupied with where his possessions, clean, restored, well-kept, as well as his body exudate would go after he dies, and was fascinated with the Egyptians, especially Tutankhamen who took all his gold and other possessions to the grave with him. Those concerns were evident also in Dr. D's attachment to such memorabilia as the man who was immortalized in Madame Tusseaud's wax museum with his preserved nails and hair put into the wax figure that was made into an exact replica of himself. This fascination relates to his preoccupations with his own feces and nasal exudate, both of which suggest an obsessional interest in inanimate matter that is infinitely regenerable. His compulsive surgical cleaning, repairing, and rebuilding were related, in that he believed that the cleaned out rot, flesh, and blood participated in the life-death cycle of appearance and disappearance with each procedural cleaning-out. These preoccupations sometimes verged on the macabre, as when a close relative died. He would not leave the hospital where she died nor take his eyes off the corpse until the morticians came. He waited for them for hours although his presence was in no way required. After the cremation, he held onto the remains, obsessed with what substances other than ashes, such as teeth and bone remnants, might be in the urn. He had been unable to get rid of the cremated remains, mainly because he took so to heart the symbolic meaning of whatever place he might have chosen to dispose of them. Thoughts of disposal were associated with other thoughts, mainly of the cremated gas-chamber victims whose gold teeth fillings stand as mementos in holocaust museums. He longed to plant his relative's ashes in his garden, as though they would grow to full fruition as he wished would happen to him after his own death. These fantasies contained elements of resurrection symbolism to be found in artistic renditions of themes of both the Resurrection of the Dead and Christ's Resurrection.

Because Dr. D customarily and energetically invaded with potentially lethal instruments, body parts and orifices generally regarded as forbidden territory, his compulsive surgical cleaning and the compulsive cleaning out of his own fecal matter can be regarded as compromise formations. Good hygienic practices would realistically guarantee a longer life, permitting as well a continuous invasion, for purposes of pleasure, of the forbidden depths of the body and what they symbolize, perhaps mother earth. The very same behavior also represented a purification ritual to pacify the superego following these frequent forays into forbidden spaces.

Additional manifestations of his yearning to penetrate forbidden places proliferated transferentially, as he would intrusively pick up things to read from my desk, always curious about my private life. Extra-transferentially, these invasive longings took the lifelong form of an obsession to go to Africa, the dark and forbidden continent. As with his literal sexual activity, his fatal attractions, this obsession with symbolically penetrating the forbidden woman was so overriding that with good opportunities to take the trip, he found reasons not to be able to go. Often, the rationalizations boiled down to a fear that any journey was to be his last, and in his neurotic efforts to ward off death and extend his life, he superstitiously avoided traveling to all the places that were, in his mind, associated with oedipal transgressions as well preoedipal fears of the engulfing, forbidden maternal object—the femme fatale.

In sum, all of the eccentric habits in relation to the decayed and the inanimate seemed to be expressing a simple message: each gesture, each flower planted, each operation of flesh cleaned and repaired, the self-scrubbing during and after each surgical intervention and each bowel movement, each day of work, each postponement of taking a trip, each instance of sexual intercourse—all were equated with extending his life by another day, culminating in his desperate and absurd attempts to postpone the end of his life indefinitely, or at the very least, to avoid the bad death. Thus, he sought to increase the chances of being resurrected in the minds of others, if only to be remembered for his eccentricities, which he deemed to be singular, unique. It was indeed amazing how his facial mien actually reflected his eccentric death and rebirth preoccupations, and at times invited attention and commentary. Typical reactions were such incidents as a man stopping him in the street, whispering, "You look like death warmed over," or a man outside a movie house saying, "You're not supposed to be alive again yet."

A psychoanalytic interpretation of Dr. D's pathological concerns with decay, exhuming, and perpetuity would, in addition to the compromise formation described earlier, also have to address the condensation of multiple fantasies in any particular enactment. In his wish for a perpetual renewal of body parts, his body itself and what goes in and out are representations of himself, whether of the body phallus, or variations on the body fecal column. This fantasy of perpetual renewal via the incorporation into himself of outside bits and pieces expresses a compromise between both fecal and castration anxiety on the one hand, and making reparation for the anticipated loss of representations of himself either as a whole or by parts. When he referred to meat-eating as "eating the body parts of animals" and as devouring raw flesh, he was expressing an aspect of this fantasy. I would designate this resurrection-fantasy variant as belonging in the general category of "parthenogenesis," or fertilizing and giving birth to a representation of oneself without benefit of intercourse with the opposite sex. Much in this resurrection fantasy with its oral incorporative and phallic narcissistic components reflected a conscious wish. The fantasy is narcissistic, to repeat, in that the parthenogenetic wish involved a drive to recreate himself without connection to a specific object, or woman. The femme fatale is simply a means to this cosmic end: a "sex object."

To repeat, these fantasies were conscious. It was the gratification of oral and anal sadistic wishes that were unconscious. It should not be forgotten that he chose surgery as a profession, one in which he could perpetually repair decay in his elderly patients, over whose bodies he had complete control to open, invade, exhume, and resurrect. So, his forbidden "fatal" sexuality found its parallel in his other obsessions and compulsions. Clearly, his concerns were to ward off the bad death and not to seek the good one. Reunion and merger fantasies with another were not part of his aim, which appeared restricted to perpetuating himself, narcissistically, in perpetuity. He would ruminate about the way precious substances are decanted out of purified waste matter, destined to be resurrected as eternal substances in our streams, rivers, oceans, and evaporating into the atmosphere, and are bound to be breathed in or ingested and renewed, perpetually, in some bond of cosmic oneness between the universe and man, particularly himself. This narcissistic variant of a resurrection fantasy, then, would appear to exclude the elements of the Liebestod as I understand the latter class of fantasy: it is not concerned with the good death via reunion and merger with an object where two are as one. Instead, the incidental object is purely instrumental in attaining the narcissistic goal of avoiding the bad death. In that sense, it would appear to reflect more pathology than a universal wish for oneness with a loved one or the cosmos in an eternal good death.

Leitmotifs of Gardening and Resurrection

> As the years went by and age overtook her, there was something
> comical yet touching in her bedraggled appearance on this awesome
> occasion—the small hunched over figure, her studied absorption in
> the implausible notion that there would be yet another spring, oblivi-
> ous to the ending of her own days which she knew perfectly well was
> near at hand, sitting there with her detailed chart under those dark
> skies, in the dying October, calmly plotting the resurrection.
> —E. B. White, Introduction to Katharine S. White's
> *Onward and Upward in the Garden*

It would be natural, after considerations of perpetuity, decay and
exhuming, to look to Dr. D's passion for gardening as a concrete
representation of these and other resurrection wishes. As close an
illustration of the erection-resurrection equation as one might expect
to encounter could be interpreted from the conscious fantasies that
he entertained in connection with a most significant portion of his
avocational "oeuvre," his garden, and what it represented in his
psyche.

By way of introduction to Dr. D's gardening obsession, I return
once more to Lifton (1979) on immortality. In speaking of the "natural mode" of immortality, Lifton referred in a footnote to

> the longstanding Anglo Saxon preoccupation with vigorously con-
> fronting the infinite dimension of nature and with "cultivating one's
> garden." In that last image, the idea of nurturing and communing with
> one's own small plot of land becomes a metaphor for tending to one's
> own realm, whether of domestic national policy or the individual
> psyche. (23)

Dr. D longed to have his ashes, after cremation, planted in his garden,
where, somehow, they would help fertilize and promote the growth
of a rose bush which, in his fantasy, would be no less than himself,
reborn. Not only did he obsessively tend his garden, he would steal
seedlings from other places to make it the best ever. On occasion he
committed the reverse infraction. When he would see a plot of some-

one else's land unplanted, he would dig up the barren earth under cover of darkness and plant something on the property he had trespassed, excited over both the idea of violation and of promoting fecundity. He would then replace the soil, as though in mimicry of both a burial and a rebirth. He became obsessed with who would tend and perpetuate his garden when he dies, and wrote and rewrote his will so that now his wife, now his children, would inherit it, depending on who he thought would most likely preserve it exactly as he had cultivated it. He had even considered willing it as land in the public trust as a memorial to himself, where he would request burial, his monument to be the rose bush that would rise from the soil, fertilized by his cremated ashes. The fantasy ended with his wife looking at the thorns in the bush, wistful about the various women whom he had penetrated sexually during his life, and who are now passing by his flowery reincarnation. As each woman leans to touch the thorny bush, his wife puns to the assembled tribute-payers, "Pricked by D again." So his gardening represented digging and exhuming his own grave in preparation for his resurrection as a phallus-prick, eternally active, sexually.

Once again, as in his vocational work of surgery, there seemed to be echoes of wishes to invade forbidden places, like the dark continent, Africa, and wishes to remain phallically erect after death, wishes that in large measure accounted for his pattern of passionate fatal attractions. His gardening mania condensed ideas about death and rebirth to a life of perpetual erection and romance. In this one man's version of the erection-resurrection equation, a gardening mania condensed many late-life preoccupations with intercourse, fathering, and generativity in general. He showed the same passionate zeal in his death-defying gardening as in his "fatal" sexual encounters.

Steinberg (1983) said that according to legend, the Tree of Life planted in the Garden of Eden was predestined to yield its wood to the cross. He was referring here to the 1511 Baldung Grien woodcut *The Fall of Man* in which we see a dead tree hosting a vigorous vine, which Steinberg called "a rectifying fresh vine that mounts the dry trunk behind St. Anne" (118). Such an interpretation would have Adam resurrected as Christ, as the Fall prefigures the Passion. The iconology that informs most art historians' interpretations of Grien's imagery does not lead generally to the kinds of conclusions that are customarily drawn in psychoanalytic interpretations of the dynamic unconscious. Those very images and what they symbolize in primary process thinking, however, would appear to have an important point of contact with Dr. D's fantasies of rebirth as a tree. Dr. D became obsessed with planting trees, each a memorial to himself; he wanted to take home a small tree in my office in order to repot it and then return it so as to guarantee him immortality, by at least serving as a reminder to me of his existence, ensuring his place in my thoughts about him. His continual planting, whether in his own or others' gardens, appeared to express nothing of the frequently encountered romantic theme of the red rose and the green briar that entwines in a true lovers' knot—a fantasized reunion *with an object* after death. Dr. D's fantasy was, rather, a self-preoccupied image of a loner, of solitary perfection, risen, on a stake, akin to one of many possible psychoanalytic readings of Grien's imagery as autonomous text: a narcissistic fantasy of the body-self as phallus, of perpetual erection memorialized into perpetuity.

A resurrection fantasy of coming back to life by growing out of the very soil of one's burial and birth place seemed in Dr. D's case to be a reaction to early but traumatic awareness of death, decomposition, and mortality which he dated to an organized memory of himself at age seventeen. It was then that he wrote a story of an old man contentedly warmed by the rays of the sun while sitting on a park bench. The indigent man was destined for interment in Potter's Field, and the adolescent writer concluded with the line, "Too bad they can't bury you exactly where you die, where the good things happen." In later life, of course, the good happening was to be "dying in the saddle."

Leitmotifs of Oral Incorporation and Phallic Parthenogenesis

Before elaborating further on the phallic-narcissistic elements which, as we have seen, are to be found frequently in the way that resurrection ideation figured in Dr. D's fantasy life, I should like to note the elements of oral incorporation that also played their part in motivating the vocational and avocational interests he pursued so intensely. In keeping with Oremland's (1989) notion that ideas of oral incorporation, or of taking-in aspects of another that enhance one's narcissism, play an important part in resurrection fantasies, it can be shown that Dr. D also thought that a greedy taking-in of the good that others possess could guarantee him immortal recognition.

His fear/wish of dying in the saddle and the related envy, anger, and degradation of women also related to his ever-desperate but failed attempts to recreate himself, parthenogenetically, with absolutely no dependence on a woman, as in trying vainly to take control of his childrens' lives by pouring all the world's knowledge from his head into theirs. However, in a particular fantasy variant of oral incorporation, that of parthenogenesis, the emphasis on narcissistic concerns is more prominent. In a typical parthenogenetic fantasy, a man wishes to perpetuate himself without benefit of intercourse with a woman, consistent with negative oedipal longings. Oremland (1989) in particular emphasizes the oral incorporative elements in his exegesis of the resurrection motifs in Michelangelo's Sistine Chapel ceiling. Like Steinberg, Oremland, basing his inferences upon Michelangelo's Sistine ceiling images, interprets Adam's parthenogenetic birth and the Fall as prefiguring Christ's immaculate conception and crucifixion, and also interprets Christ's resurrection as a continuation of Adam's life on earth. Oremland holds that oral incorporation motifs inhere in resurrection ideation which always implies a wish to perpetuate a lost object by taking it into the self, as the self becomes perpetuated by being taken into others, ad infinitum, into perpetuity. He notes the parthenogenetic, particularly the auto-fellatio aspects of oral incorporation in several Sistine Chapel images of self-fertilization, birth, and rebirth.

On the day that Dr. D expressed a wish for me to look at and take in as fully as he had Katharine White's book (1981) with its explicit reference to gardening and resurrection, he expressed greed to "eat up" everything written. He was sure that I knew everything there was to know about psychoanalysis and it was just a matter of my discretion when I would pour it all into his head. He would then be in a position to pour all of his ingested knowledge into the head of his grandchild and all of his professional knowledge into the head of whichever young man was to replace him in his practice. However, to recreate himself by transferring his wealth to a chosen individual in the next generation led to conflict because it was contingent on his dying. Many of his unconscious fantasies and conflicts were based on cannibalistic wishes to devour another person's power, and on the wish to resurrect himself in the image of the all-knowing one whose phallic power he has incorporated, orally. This form of greed is precisely what motivated his relationship to the mentor whose practice he had bought out early in his own career. When the older man did not die as soon as Dr. D anticipated, Dr. D harbored murderous wishes toward him, and because he anticipated similar motives on the part of whomever was to buy out his practice prior to his retirement, his fear of being drained by his successor alternated with oral expulsion wishes to pour everything he knew into his replacement. The conflict led to paralysis of his will in arranging for someone to buy out his practice in preparation for retirement. Related are marked filicidal fantasies toward his own children, fueled by his projections onto them of his wishes to steal and then incorporate the paternal phallus. Dr. D at times seemed concerned about their well-being after his death, but was tormented by ideas of how they would probably misappropriate and abuse his possessions, unable to love and cherish them with an intensity equal to his own. In retaliation for the parricidal treachery he expected from them, he disappropriated his children from time to time in impulsive rewritings of his will. His projections onto them paralleled a disregard for his own father after the latter's death. It would be just as futile to expect that his children would be the ones to resurrect him as it was futile to believe he wanted to resurrect his own father.

While my focus here is on the oral incorporative elements of resurrection fantasies, these wishes also contain clearly negative oedipal and homosexual implications, as in Dr. D's wish to orally incorporate the idealized parental phallus. In keeping with his negative oedipal fantasies of submission to a powerful but benevolent father, is Dr. D's expressed "nostalgia" for Renaissance art history, the time when such artists as Michelangelo had patrons. He had the conscious fantasy of making himself the favored "pet" of senior members of his profession who would patronize him, and whose practices he dreamed of inheriting upon their deaths in return for the favor of his obsequies. As I mentioned earlier, he lived out his Renaissance man fantasies, taking for granted his unusual attractiveness, skills, and knowledge. I should interject here that in a pathographical consideration of the psychological determinants that may have influenced the individual Florentine artists' paintings of certain images, such as the father's hand on the groin of the dead son, we may be onto something beyond the Christological creed as understood by Steinberg. I am referring to the breakthrough of homosexual, negative oedipal thematic material that might well have been very prominent in the personal lives of many of the Florentine painters who thrived in the patronage system just as it was prominent in Dr. D's living-out of his idiosyncratic patronage fantasies.

As termination of his analysis drew near, Dr. D seemed to be experiencing that ending in the very terms of impending death: each new session represented to him a chance to buy more time to live. He fantasized having the wisdom of all my books and all the books ever written on psychoanalysis poured into him as I, in the transference, represented the paternal phallus to be incorporated and then passed on. The desperation for me to read his gardening book with its reference to resurrection suggested to me that because he knew of my interest in writing, he may have wanted me to immortalize him in a book. He denied this, but did imagine I might write up my case to present to my classes, making of his case history the immortalizing biography he had always dreamed about. It was as though he wanted me to eat his book and thereby incorporate him, keeping him with me after his death, just as he wished to pour knowledge down the throats of his issue. There was a poignancy in his wish to have me eat, preserve, and resurrect him in myself, sexually as well. He felt a sense of sexual excitement as he cannibalistically ingested the world's art into himself and then poured it into a woman so that she would impress his image upon her father and sons, thereby guaranteeing his resurrection in the minds of those who were vitally important to him.

Leitmotifs of Phallic Body Narcissism

Most of the psychoanalytic literature on death preoccupations gives priority to fantasies of rebirth, reunion, and merger with a lost other and provides lesser emphasis on the phallic narcissistic aspects of resurrection via self-perpetuity. Blacker (1983) believes that the idea of rebirth indicates starting life anew without blemish, whereas resurrection fantasies express the wish for another chance to live but with the same defective body. The idea of defect and the phallic castration anxieties underlying it, are at the root of many of Dr. D's resurrection fantasies. His self-image as an immortalized body-phallus is evocative of Steinberg's erection-resurrection equation, and his preoccupation with immortality and resurrection cannot be understood readily in terms of merger with the lost object. That his resurrection fantasies are more narcissistic than object-related was noted earlier, in connection with his wish to reincarnate as a lone rose bush, not as one entwining with the green briar. There is a conspicuous absence of an other in his resurrection fantasies, with the exception of the mirroring audience, a selfobject (Kohut). This patient sustained no significant early losses and no significant early identifications with a lost object. He did, however, experience significant narcissistic losses, both of his physical prowess and attractiveness and of living up to a perfectionistic and esteemed idealized self-image. In his case, one may speak of identifications with a lost part-object, the phallus, as opposed to the loss of a whole person, as his ideas of death related primarily to detumescence, while those of tumescence represent the coming to life again. I did learn late in the treatment that his mother had been hospitalized in a psychiatric hospital for "premature senility" and his preoccupations could be seen in part as a late-life identification with her during her waning years. Mostly, though, his fantasies were narcissistic dreams of glory and everlasting sexual and artistic might.

Dr. D wished he could be a character in a Molière play where everyone is around his deathbed (see figure 16) and, unbeknownst to them, he comes back to life to hear what they have to say about him. He, like Blacker, but for different reasons, was intrigued by people who had died, technically speaking, and then come back to life, as after cardiac arrest or in drowning and resuscitation. Themes of the raising of the dead and the curing of cripples, such as those that appear in Renaissance art, fascinated him. He hoped that he might upon his death achieve a moment of peace, representing the alleged transmigration of souls.

The patient, the would-be-artist, felt convinced that there was a special connection between Picasso's creativity, his longevity, and his phallic preoccupations. Picasso was Dr. D's ego ideal, because the artist lived to a ripe old age. Dr. D was convinced that an obscene enjoyment of perverse and illicit sex in his old age permitted Picasso his immortal fame. The lascivious content of the artist's perpetually surviving paintings, particularly those painted in old age, were a sign to this patient that Picasso's active sexual life promoted both his art and his immortality. Because Dr. D did not possess Picasso's artistic gifts, and because he found his sexual activity to be on the wane, he felt less likely to be immortalized in glorious ways, and was more and more preoccupied with avoiding the unwelcome fate of a "bad death," of the humiliating death of fading into insignificance and oblivion. He therefore resorted, sometimes consciously, sometimes unconsciously, to various measures that were intended to ward off the bad death, measures which, as he got older, were stepped up with a drivenness and intensity, followed by frustration. It was the chronic and cyclical nature of these swings that lent the stamp of the pathological to an otherwise normal phase in the life cycle.

One special way that Dr. D attempted to ward off death was to buy clothes, endlessly, the unconscious fantasy being that each newly purchased garment buys an extra day of life. He was obsessed each morning with how to put together a unique ensemble. There was never any repetition of shirt, pants, sweater, and jacket combinations, or of any given color combination. That would be the death of him. When I quipped that we ought to get him together with Imelda Marcos, he remained serious, convinced that she replenished her

Figure 16. The artist's fantasy of a sublimated "dying in the saddle," in which everyone surrounds his deathbed, immortalizing his sexual prowess. (Sir Edward Burne-Jones, *Arthur in Avalon*, detail [1881–98]. Museo de Arte, Ponce, Puerto Rico. Bridgeman/Art Resource, New York.)

stocks, aiming for an unlimited supply of shoes because she knew she could not possibly get around to wearing everything, thus expressing her effort to stay alive, forever. It is of interest that he was bequeathed, and nostalgically cherished, the overcoat of his most adored patient, a man famous as a patron of the arts.

Dr. D in fact compulsively collected shirts and pants to hang in his closet as he got older, unconsciously believing that each article of clothing wards off death as it extends his life and promotes a phallic self-image. Shortly following a point at which new purchases became a near daily affair, he lapsed into a depression at the thought that his wife might, after his death, donate the garments to a thrift shop where, in the patient's words, "they would hang limp like a dead, detumescent penis." If his sons, the fruit of his loins, would only inherit the garments and wear them, he would have some hope of resurrecting himself, his immortality guaranteed. Dr. D's worst fears were that his sons would discard the clothing as being too big for them to fill out, and he literally imagined himself sentenced to that fate of hanging limp in a thrift shop.

The leitmotifs of phallic narcissism and of immortality could be discerned in the patient's chronic bouts of insomnia when he would sit up, refuse to prepare for bed, and then attempt to reassure himself by compulsively masturbating, falling asleep erect or at the table, all the while attempting to maintain a phallic-erect posture. One reason he gave for fear of going to sleep, and particularly of sleeping lying down in bed, is that he would wake up without his habitual morning erection, and he wanted to avoid facing that disturbing event. Here, we see a literal enactment of a resurrection wish via concrete behavioral and postural representations of the body phallus, where the state of arousal functions as a defense against some wish to be eaten, to fall asleep, and to die a death merged with his wife in their marriage bed. For Dr. D, such merger which to many individuals would epitomize the "good death" connoted only the bad. Therefore, he counterphobically avoided the possibility of losing the firm self-feeling of imagining the body as a phallus: he avoided any attempt at intercourse that might lead to a lost erection, for he unconsciously equated the normal detumescence, and the relaxation and sleep following orgasm with being merged with, identified with, and transformed into a woman.

These profound castration and merger anxieties were echoed in Dr. D's fantasy of a primal, guiltless, perpetual erection. He started his analysis by elaborating on a fantasy that he had made a bargain with the devil to extend his life, indefinitely. He was willing to go to hell and suffer all the torments if in his perpetual life he could enjoy a very exciting, even terrifying sexuality. As he aged, however, he was guilt-ridden to the point of abstinence dictated by growing fears of impotence and death.

His sexual life took on more and more of a masochistic coloring as he advanced in years. Bondage and beating scenarios were enacted in actual sexual encounters, and could be discerned as unconscious motivators of some of his more eccentric habits. In his illicit affairs, he often consciously fantasized a flagellation, even asked to have his hands tied, "like Christ on the Cross." When he fantasized his flagellation and crucifixion, he would get a "tremendous erection" and then he overtly fantasized about "dying in the saddle, what a way to go." Such fantasies suggest the connection between crucifixion fantasies and beating fantasies proposed by Edelheit (1974). For this particular patient, the fantasies seemed to increase his feeling of differentiation from the potentially dangerous woman of merger and to increase the phallic narcissistic body feeling as a defense against castration anxiety.

Concluding Remarks

Freud (1926) said that the conscious fear of death, in addition to signifying the fear of castration, condenses all the danger situations as well as signifying failures in the protective shield, as when excessive amounts of excitation impinge upon the mental apparatus. There is no doubt that Dr. D scared himself with the overstimulation of excessive excitement which he felt put him constantly in danger of being abandoned by the powers-that-be, upon whom he depended. These conscious fears gratified his masochism and blended into flagellation and crucifixion fantasies with an increasing identification with the figure of Christ in the Passion of his last days. We recall in this connection the patient's illicit activities in the army, some of which violated his professional vows, and his extramarital indiscretions that risked considerable moral approbation, or so he thought. Death, with its particular unconscious meaning of castration, was to be a punishment for a lifelong accumulation of literal and symbolically illicit actions, the latter including his very career. He considered his courses in anatomy and pathology to be the ecstatic pinnacle of his training and could not imagine how they could be anything but thrillingly pleasant to anyone lucky enough to have had the experience of dissecting a cadaver. He feared discovery, however, for having performed an illicit excavation, of penetrating the dark and forbidden continent with any slip of his scalpel or other surgical equipment. Freud (1915) also said that we dare not contemplate a great many undertakings which are dangerous but in fact indispensable, such as attempts at artificial flight, expeditions to distant countries, or experiments with explosive substances. Indeed, it was with the onset of conscious death anxieties that my patient stopped all travels, which he formerly loved as among his favorite illicit preoccupations, tied in not just with literal violations of sexual mores but with the symbolic invading of the territories of forbidden bodies of land and other space.

Dr. D was constantly on guard about being found out, usually for he knew not what. One of his most terrifying moments came on the occasion of his being audited by the Internal Revenue Service. Although in fact not guilty of any of the tax violations under investigation, he feared that his tax-deductible fees paid to me over the years would be deemed illegal and that he would be jailed or professionally admonished so as to be unable to work again. That is, he masochistically fantasized taking a beating from me for his transferential feelings, as he made not too subtle but very provocative attempts at introducing tones of illicitness into the treatment. For example, he had begun woefully pleading to me, using my first name, to complain about his wife's lack of understanding. He attempted to woo me in this stylized manner as he had wooed in all of his extramarital relationships. What the IRS was doing was in fact tantamount to no more than a slap on the wrist (he had listed one large personal liquor bill as a professional expense), but he would use these slaps to gratify beating fantasies, working himself up into a chronic anticipation of the worst possible type of punishment—his version of the flagellation and the crucifixion. These doom anxieties were related to his neurotic fears of poverty, as though when the supply of money, clothes, garden innovations, and most important, the treatment itself would run out, he would die.

It is of interest that Dr. D had been preoccupied with circumcision and its connection with extended or aborted life spans. He remembered vividly a World War II incident in which the Germans asked a group of French hostages to pull down their pants, whereupon they killed all of the circumcised, presumably Jewish men, in a terrible blood bath. A dramatic incident related to these preoccupations occurred during the first few weeks of his treatment, when I noticed a trickle of blood seeping through his trousers around the groin area. His explanation was that he had to run to get to his appointment with me promptly, knowing he would be charged and chastised for the missed time, and in his haste he collided with an open taxi door which ripped his flesh, later requiring seventeen stitches to repair. During the session, he endured his pain, martyred yet proud of his ability to bear it. It was not until later in the analysis that he was able to associate the blood to the blood on Christ's groin in Renaissance paintings. This in turn related to the many beating, flagellation, and crucifixion fantasies he had, and to his comparison of the blood signifying life to the bloodless death state he feared. One might well conclude, based on a pathographical study of Dr. D's "oeuvre," that the circumcision prefigures the resurrection not only in art but in life as well.

The analysis of Dr. D ended on a note of highlighted Liebestod and resurrection fantasies combined. Although he gave up the dangerous death-dealing fatal attraction that brought him to treatment in the first place, he replaced that enactment with a newer version of his fantasies. It was his wish that his analyst resurrect him in memory through a biographical narrative study to become part of the psychoanalytic literature. Did the analyst, too, drawn to the stories of fatal attraction of the Liebestod and the Resurrection, share many fantasies in common with her analysand, wishing, as he did, that their joint endeavors be resurrected through "immortal" preservation, analogous to the way a work is preserved in a museum? Being "fatally" attracted to their work, they thus transform the fatal to the eternally viable, and hopefully, the pathological to the normative.

Seven

Detecting Pathological Variants of Resurrection Fantasies

*T*he Case of Dr. D and other material that I have presented is intended to highlight the universal fantasies
shared by certain lovers throughout the ages, and by artists and their
audiences whose imaginations have been captured by themes of love,
death, and the fatal attractions of the Liebestod and resurrection
imagery. At this point in my study of resurrection fantasies, I will try
to sort out the normative and the pathological by thematic analyses
in two separate but parallel realms: universally based psychological
fantasies, and theologically and historically based images. Resurrection themes in art images may be interpreted along similar lines to
those in individual fantasy life, even though we cannot assume pathology in the art images per se, as they are essentially symbols and
metaphors. In a study of resurrection fantasies and motifs, universal
psychological elements, and theological elements embraced by large
social groups in one given historical context such as the Renaissance,
signify that we are dealing with normative aspects of the fantasies.
When we find idiosyncratic rather than universal elements in the
fantasies of artists and audiences, as well as those expressed in art
which are motifs (images, themes) not embraced by a particular
iconographical tradition or by a particular theological or sociological

reading, we are likely to be are stepping out of the normative and into the pathological realm. Universal psychological fantasies and iconographic traditions would underscore the normative; idiosyncratic renderings would signify the pathological. It is of course true that certain iconographic traditions make use of preexisting universal unconscious fantasies. Nevertheless, it is necessary for the interpreter of art images to be informed as to whether a particular tradition of pictorial representation of a theme is characteristic or whether it is idiosyncratic before offering a psychological interpretation suggesting that the artist has expressed a pathological variant of a universal fantasy.

This section aims to highlight some of the universal fantasies underlying the psychological normative, as well as the socio-theological traditions underlying the historical normative. It must be born in mind, however, that just because a given product has as its roots the psychological and the historical normative, there can also be pathological variants. Let us consider an example of an iconographic tradition which, though not an example of resurrection imagery, would confront us with the task of sorting out the theological from psychological themes. Steinberg noted that the Magi in many nativity scenes are staring at the exposed genitals of the Christ child. In Renaissance Florence, as well as throughout the civilized world up until the present time, doctors and wise men have checked out the body parts of the newborn in order to determine that everything is in place. From the point of view of historical tradition, it would not be appropriate to interpret most Nativity scenes as portraying exhibitionistic-voyeuristic behavior. Gazing at the child's genitals would not necessarily reflect phallic preoccupations in Renaissance times, as it would in other times and places. Our interpretation of the images, guided by the theology of the time, would tend toward seeing the gaze as a sign of marveling at the incarnation of God in the person of the baby Jesus. In certain instances, however, as when the rendition is idiosyncratic and does not follow the iconographic traditions of the time, it would be reasonable to interpret that the artist has captured in his imagery a phallic-exhibitionistic-voyeuristic fantasy and is consciously or unconsciously reaching out to stimulate that same fantasy in his audience.

The equation of erection with resurrection undoubtedly resonates with similar themes embodied in ancient mythology, in presently embraced theologies, in iconography, and in all human minds as well. Thus, there must be something other than the Christian theology of incarnation and humanation in the fantasy of perpetual erection that is connected with ideas of resurrection. Most important, these fantasies, because they are universal, must have captured the imagination of preacher, painter, and audience alike. If an audience viewing a particular painting were to put itself in the painter's place, empathically, it would appreciatively receive the unconscious messages conveyed by the artist through his or her pictures. It is in just such an identifying audience that we would find Dr. D, the would-be-artist who takes as his ego ideal the bona fide artist, Picasso, who produces immortal works. Dr. D, whose erection-resurrection fantasies presumably were activated by similar fantasies on the part of the painter, idealized the erotica that characterized the artist's oeuvre in the last decade of his life, in his nineties. Indeed, in the manifest context of Picasso's work are to be found abundant and undisguised representations of tumescent genitals. It is legitimate to attempt a pathographic reading of Picasso's work as yielding a clear connection between direct and symbolic renditions of erection and that artist's personal preoccupations with his own impending death and with immortality fantasies. This connection comes as close as any to a direct and not always symbolically disguised erection-resurrection equation. Here, the parallels in the artist's fantasy, as depicted in his paintings, and Dr. D's fantasies are so bluntly evident as to make unremarkable Steinberg's thesis (1983), often thought to be radical and sacrilegious-sounding. Steinberg was dealing simply with the historical-theological norms of a certain time. However, the noniconographic renderings of Picasso and the idiosyncratic behavior of Dr. D permit an interpretation of nonnormative and therefore possibly psychopathological elements.

Over time, similar versions of certain universal fantasies will be discernible in a wide variety of contexts via a variety of interpretive approaches. We may discern these similarities when we interpret a work of art thematically or as an autonomous text, that is, on its own terms, as when there is no psychobiographical information about the artist at our disposal to permit a pathographic investigation. When we do have such information and apply to that work of art the pathographic method with its focus on the oeuvre and on the life of the artist who created the work, we may also uncover aspects of universal as well as idiosyncratic fantasies. We may discern those same fantasies in such patients as Dr. D, whom we study psychoanalytically. Elements common to all of these contexts may be interpreted similarly. This approach does not deny time- and place-bound factors that, along with universal fantasies, also determine the final outcome of art or of personality. The traditions and customs of a certain place and time, such as trecento and quattrocento Florence, indeed were woven into the iconographical traditions and subsequent renderings of Italian Renaissance paintings, just as twentieth-century fashions influenced Dr. D's acquisition of skills and the arenas he chose for their expression. We should not be constrained, however, by an either/or approach which would have us interpret the meaning of a painting as reflecting on the one hand only local fifteenth-century iconographical tradition, that is, the normative for the time, or on the other hand, only the unconscious fantasies of the creating artist and of the people constituting the aesthetically experiencing audience. However, we must know something of *both* the normative time-bound and the normative universal in order to distinguish those factors from the idiosyncratic and pathological variants, both psychological and socio-historical.

As for resurrection fantasies in life and art, Steinberg's erection-resurrection equation comes close to an appreciation of the interface of psychoanalytic and iconographical traditions that inform paintings, even though he disavows any intention to approach art with the psychoanalyst's focus on universal contents in the dynamic unconscious. The multitude of examples he has collected of penile erection in the risen Christ is meant to illustrate the iconographic traditions informed by the Christian theology of the Renaissance. He explicitly intended to shed light on the theological-historical normative, claiming that his methodology has no power to unearth the pathological. Yet, a psychoanalyst looking at the same data through the lens of the psychological-symbolic would undoubtedly uncover a multitude of underlying motivational factors and universal normative fantasies with certain psychological variants. Steinberg's main thesis of the erection-resurrection equation aims to demonstrate that there are primarily theological grounds to account for suggestions of the sexuality of Christ in the pictorial imagery of his exposed, tumescent genitals, and that there are mainly political-theological grounds deriving from the formal censorship by the Church introduced at the Council of Trent to account for the later oblivion to which such obvious sexual imagery had become relegated. He never proposed that psychological censorship, or repression, could also account for the disappearance of Christ's sexuality in post-Renaissance art. In elaborating the meaning of images of unveiled genitalia in art works depicting the resurrection, Steinberg invoked only explanations deriving from the Renaissance incarnational *theology*. He rejected a psychological explanation, or the idea that primal fantasies inform theology. However, he did note that post-Renaissance Christians from the latter sixteenth century onward saw as shocking the genital exposure and unveiling in Renaissance paintings, while individuals living during the Renaissance did not. After the late 1500s and the Council of Trent, the Christian community disallowed direct reference to the sexual member of Christ, resorting to veils and overpainting of the original Renaissance canvasses, culminating in the oblivion of which Steinberg speaks. Steinberg, however, cannot justifiably avoid reliance on the concept of psychological censorship, including repression, to help explain the process and signs of this oblivion. He did not propose *both* theological and psychological grounds to account for a *motivated* appearance or disappearance of sexuality in the manifest content of Renaissance art renditions of the Christ story. It is difficult to understand why Steinberg could not accommodate a multiperspectival approach which would allow both sets of factors to codetermine the form and content of the expressive art work. The theological and the psychological are indeed interwoven in commonly shared human fantasies that motivate the artist to create the images and the audience to appreciate them.

In his emphasis on the normative historical-theological, Steinberg attempted to grasp the flux of meanings over time in one given art image. He felt that signs of penile erection in Renaissance paintings of the resurrected Christ would require that the erection-resurrection equation in the risen Christ be interpreted primarily in terms of the theology of the time, that is, the incarnation of the man who is to be God, and not in terms of a wish for permanent erection or any of the other universal themes, psychological or otherwise, which this image might, as the normative-psychological, signify at any time in history. Steinberg correctly argued that as far as signs and new meanings go, we should indeed pay attention to time-bound iconology, but even with proper regard for contextual changes of meaning in time and place, we should never lose sight of psychological timelessness in our effort to grasp certain unconscious universal meanings of symbols. The psychological approach, as well as the iconographic, may lead to an uncovering of universal and therefore normative meanings.

An Italian Renaissance painter who painted a Resurrection scene according prominence to the *genitalia ostentatio,* as in the example cited earlier, in chapter 5, of the obvious erections discerned beneath the loincloth of Christ rising, may have been making a theologically based iconographic statement, conscious and deliberate. How can we tell if the individual artist was also motivated in this depiction by an idiosyncratic resurrection fantasy expressing certain pathological elements of his personality? One way would be to apply the pathographic method to the artist's life and work. When there is no access to the data that make this method feasible, we can still validly say, psychoanalytically speaking, that iconographical traditions informing Renaissance paintings of the Resurrection which call our attention to Christ's genitalia resonate with unconscious fantasies that we do have access to in many people. Other fantasies stimulated by viewing images of Christ's dead body resurrected involve, as Binion's (1993) examples suggest, an eroticization of Christ's death, typically seen in certain nineteenth-century depictions of deadly sex and terminal ecstasies. He cites two unquestionable examples of such fantasies. One is that of Mirabeau's gay priest who would daydream: "To run one's repentant lips over that adorable body, to press one's mouth against the gaping wounds in those aching thighs, to kiss the broken limbs, to feel that heavenly flesh burn against one's mortal flesh" (Binion 1993, 87, after Sebastion Roch 1890). Another is that of the blasphemous couple who "aligned their caresses with Christ's agony, replicating by turns 'the kiss of thorns, the touch of the leached lashes, the cherished bite of the nails, the carnal penetration of the lance, the spasms of death, the joys of decay' " (Binion 87, after Gourmand's 1891 *Le Fantôme*).

In these fantasies, resurrection has an array of meanings, including phallic narcissism and voyeurism, the wish for perpetual erection or perpetual sensual pleasure, and their perverse variations. Because these fantasies are universal, or communal (Kuhns 1983), we assume them to be at least latent and potential motivators of the creating artist's product and the aesthetically experiencing viewer's repertoire of interpretive possibilities. That *that* flesh, the genitalia, is portrayed as risen, implies that an adequate interpretation of the meaning of the image relies on a common culture of communal or primal fantasies of all humanity and not on a simple linkage, as Steinberg would have it, to the theologically based conceptions, of the humanation of Christ in Renaissance art, letters, and sermons. The normative aspects of Resurrection fantasies, then, derive from their being *both* a reflection of time-bound theology and of communal or universal fantasies.

According to Steinberg, the main theological theme in all Renaissance art is the humanation of God, the incarnation, divinity investing itself in the infirmity of the flesh. Thus, the resurrection imagery of the *genitalia ostentatio* reflects a theological message: to raise that flesh to the prerogative of immortality. So artists, in keeping with theology alone depicted human gestures consistent with this theme: the Magi staring at the babe's genitals, the Christ of the lamentation cupping his own genitals, and the resurrected Christ with visible signs of an erection beneath the loincloth.

Psychoanalysts who are interested in the relation of iconography to universal fantasy could not be too persuaded by Steinberg's elaboration of his main thesis:

Is the *ostentatio genitalium* in Renaissance images of the Christ Child in any sense cognate with the phallic cults of antiquity? Of the voluminous literature dealing with the subject of "penile display," very little, if any, bears directly on the present inquiry. To students of cultures, or of individual psychology, the phenomena of genital exhibition are familiar either as symbolic modes of aggression, or as forms of fertility worship. Neither one nor the other operates in the images under discussion—unless by inversion of traditional connotations. (1983, 46)

Here, by introducing a consideration of possibly pathological vicissitudes of sex and aggression in penile display, Steinberg argued that these pathological variants should never enter into an interpretation of what I have been calling a normative aspect of the imagery in question. The psychoanalyst, in contrast, might argue that penile display could be a manifestation of a universally found instinct or wish of exhibitionism, and that if the wish is highly conflictual and repudiated, it could be expressed in certain pathological compromise formations that we call symptoms. Exhibiting one's genitals may serve to assure that one is not castrated, or that one is a virile man, let alone human. From this point of view, and contrary to Steinberg's thesis, phallic themes with underlying meanings familiar to students of individual psychoanalytic psychology might very well operate in the images under discussion, and would then express certain pathological personality trends, such as exhibitionistic perversions. Images of genital exposure in the theologically derived incarnation themes would be understood as overdetermined, capable of being interpreted according to the rules of all disciplines, in ways that do not exclude but complement one another. Penile display in Renaissance art, then, is multiply determined, and while one determinant may be more salient in the interpretations offered, or in the meanings to be discerned at a given time in the history of theology and painting, it does seem arbitrary to exclude the latent exegetic potential of the other determinants. Further, Steinberg's idea of the inversion of traditional connotations intrigues. We are all capable of inversion, including the painters, some of whom were practicing sexual inverts.

It is difficult to believe that phallic imagery in paintings of the

Christ story can never be interpreted psychoanalytically, and that the symbols may be understood exclusively in the terms of the Renaissance theology of the humanation of Christ. Phallic images which have blood and mutilation as part of their content, such as the blood-hyphen pointing to the groin of the circumcised Christ, would have to suggest castration, or at least something more than a simple theological interpretation allows. The meaning of penile display in art images, Steinberg asserted, must be sought in the context of the Christian common creed alone, and should not be interpreted in the psychological terms of phallic symbolism:

> The sexual member exhibited by the Christ Child, so far from asserting aggressive virility, concedes instead God's assumption of human weakness; it is an affirmation not of superior prowess, but of condescension to kinship, a sign of the creator's self-abasement to his creature's condition. And instead of symbolizing, like the phallus of Dionysius, the generative powers of nature, Christ's sexual organ— pruned by circumcision in sign of corrupted nature's correction—is offered to immolation. The erstwhile symbol of the life force yields not seed but redeeming blood. (47–48)

In avoiding any psychological interpretation and remaining with the theological normative, Steinberg avoided both the normative and the pathological psychological implications of the bloody imagery of the passion. He chose to avoid any psychological interpretation. Although Steinberg noted in the blood-hyphen from the side to the groin the connection of the wounds of the Passion with the wounds of the circumcision, he denied that this imagery has phallic connotations as well, closing out on the possibility for psychoanalytic interpretation. His approach, invoking the time-bound theological is thus limited to the historically based normative of Renaissance times, and ignores the universal psychological normative, as well as the pathological psychological variants in the symbolic meanings of the genital sexual imagery, such as bleeding and penile display in the context of death and resurrection. The imagery might suggest to a psychoanalytic interpreter that a man's preoccupation with virility and phallic prowess could ward off fears of death, as it did not just in the case of the contemporary Dr. D, but in the cases of the

quintessential Renaissance artist, Michelangelo, and the more contemporary Picasso. Their sculpture and paintings may or may not
have followed the credo of the day. No matter what the conventions
for painting at a given time, no matter what received iconography
individual artists follow, the individual stamp of the artist's psyche
may be examined for the idiosyncratic fantasies it may express.

A similar conclusion may be drawn from the ample pictorial evidence that Steinberg provided for the undisguised form of *ostentatio,*
the self-touch, in which Christ is shown directly touching his groin.
The gesture of self-touch is to be found in scenes of the Man of
Sorrows, the Entombment, the Lamentation, the Deposition, and the
Pietà, in the aftermath of the Passion. Steinberg said that a dead
man's hand cupping his genitals forms no part of standard iconographic traditions, but is proper only to mid-fourteenth-century representations of Christ and later representations of Adam, and to
certain "high-dying princes and prelates whose tomb effigies rehearse
Christ's own posture" (103).

As I mentioned earlier, in chapter 5, Steinberg reasoned that since
real corpses do not move their hands to touch their groins, the artists
who depicted the dead Christ as clutching, grasping, cupping his
genitals were making Christ seem both dead and alive. Steinberg's
position on the images of the dead Christ touching his groin is
weighted too much on the side of time-bound iconography, and not
enough on the dynamic unconscious which connects with idiosyncratic and pathological as well as universal and normative fantasies,
particularly those linking death anxieties with castration anxieties.
Steinberg stated: "If personal or subconscious drives motivated this
or that artist in his approach to the Christ theme, these drives were
ultimately subordinated to his conscious grasp of the subject, since
the treatment he accorded the subject must be compatible with the
liturgical functions which the work was to serve" (107). This statement epitomizes Steinberg's position of according the bulk of the
weight to theological tradition and virtually none to unconscious
fantasy, even in interpreting overtly sexual art images. It is most
important to realize that any artist, working at any time, is under the
constraints of the conventions of the time. It is always the interpret-

er's obligation to sort out the normative aspects of the works from the idiosyncratic motives that guide any given rendition of a theme at any given time.

The subtle and bold suggestions of erection in Renaissance art do not simply reflect the time and theology-bound liturgical conventions that the works were intended to serve, but they also condense timeless mortal human fantasies, for example, castration, reunion, and rebirth, in all of their general and specific manifestations. Iconographical traditions of the Renaissance would have Christ's genital exposure as representing his incarnation. As Steinberg himself said, erection, genital gazing, and genital touching were literally erased, overpainted, prudently decked in layers of drapery and otherwise cast into oblivion. He did not believe, however, that specific conflicts about phallic sexuality motivated either the original creation of such symbols or the literal censorship imposed centuries after the paintings were created. What he did not say was that the iconographically relevant sexual symbolism that carried messages of incarnation had to be cast into oblivion by audiences who unconsciously could attribute other meanings to the symbols.

The most compelling evidence one might find for the influence of the dynamic unconscious in determining the form and content of a work of art would be from a pathographic study of an artist's work in relation to what is known about that artist's life. It might indeed turn out to be the case, on occasion, that application of the pathographic method unearths little evidence for a fantasy of perpetual eroticism, for example, as particularly salient in motivating a given artist's painting of the crucified or risen Christ with a visible sign of erection. Such an artist's rendition of the resurrection could have been motivated primarily by adherence to the theological traditions of the time, reflected in an iconography in which images of genital erection in resurrection paintings underscored the incarnational theology. Rules for interpreting the religious themes underlying the renditions of most resurrection paintings of the Italian and Northern Renaissance are typically time-bound and place-bound. In such a case, we would assign more weight to iconographical tradition than to universal latent fantasy in interpreting that particular artist's paintings. Our interest in latent, dynamically unconscious themes might be held in abeyance when there is no evidence of them from a study of the artist's life, even though psychoanalysts would be hard put not to look for latent and universal phallic-sexual castrative fantasies as also having contributed to both the iconography and an individual artist's rendition of it. However, in Michelangelo's work, about whose life we know quite a bit, the weighting might well go in the other direction: the unconscious fantasy meaning of his images would receive much more weight relative to the theological meaning than the fantasy motivations of other artists, because we know as much from pathographic studies of his personal history as it relates to his art as we do from the iconographical traditions which informed him in his unique-to-the-time renditions of Christ, particularly his unique way of representing the uncovered genitals in his nude *Christ Risen.* Whether his unconscious motivations for his pictorial representations indicate a normal or a pathological disposition is of course a matter of understanding the larger context of his life and the extent to which his art reflects sublimations and conflict resolutions.

The widespread reluctance outside of psychoanalytic circles to admit psychoanalytically based evidence into considerations of interpretations of art images is an important matter because it is still not easy to persuade certain nonpsychoanalytic art historians of the rich source much art work presents for an understanding of individual pathology as well as for nonpathological idiosyncratic psychological factors. Despite the power of evidence from psychological sources in pathographic studies, it is not unusual to hear from art historians purely culture-bound, normative explanations for such themes as analysts traditionally attribute to dynamically unconscious fantasy content. Steinberg rightly said that naturalistic motifs in religious art are "never adequately accounted for by their prevalence in life situations. Ordinary experience is no template for automatic transfer to art" (1983, 8). An example of this limited normative accounting, given earlier in this chapter, would be to understand the motifs of the Magi gazing at the Christ child's genitals as simply reflecting the fifteenth-century Florentine habit of checking out the newborn baby's body parts to ascertain that the baby is healthy. A Renaissance painter would be informed by such cultural habits, and by other art traditions, such as the direct importation of stylistic elements commonly employed in preceding centuries. Most art historians, for example, have interpreted the nudity in Michelangelo's *Dying Slave,* which Liebert saw as a culmination of the resurrection themes in his *Christ Risen,* as a direct importation of the style found in antiquity, specifically that of the Hellenistic Laocoön sculpture (100–80 B.C.). It is more accurate to think of primal fantasies as one among many templates for art, theology and cultural traditions. Liebert (1983), in his more broadly based pathographic study of Michelangelo's life and work, questioned the limitations of the more simplistic perspective, which holds the ancient source informing the formal aspects of the Laocoön group to be the sole influence on Michelangelo's statue. That statue conforms to no clearly known Renaissance iconographical tradition, and thereby opens the way for interpretations beyond the normative. Liebert argued that the Laocoön group depicting father and son bound together in an agonizing death by sea serpents, so deeply touched unconscious conflicts in Michelangelo as to make it irresistible to him as a model for his *Dying Slave.* He suggested that the union of fathers and sons in death, a theme portrayed in the ancient statue, resonated with a profound unconscious conflict in Michelangelo. These, according to Liebert, were mainly homosexual conflicts, as evidenced in the artist's reluctant submission, in a constant state of bondage to popes and other great paternal figures, in carrying through his commissions, representing himself as an innocent victim with noble intentions.

Liebert also made use of the facts of Michelangelo's personal life with young men and the artist's knowledge of mythology and of Hellenistic art, in interpreting Michelangelo's own idiosyncratic versions of a resurrection fantasy of erotized reunion with a homosexual object:

> That fantasy involved the powerful transformation of his lost early maternal figures into paternal ones. This yearning, however, carried with it the dread of bodily disintegration and castration that attended his concept of death and of fusion with the nurturing, powerful object representation, respectively. (171–72)

> For the last forty-eight years of his eighty-nine years, Michelangelo
> continually wrote and spoke of his imminent death. Clearly, this ob-
> sessive dread masked his wish to experience death as the transcenden-
> tal ecstasy suggested by the Dying Slave. (178 [italics mine])

> Michelangelo felt he could again become the son, achieving Gany-
> mede-like immortality in service and devotion to an eternally youthful
> master. . . . As one would expect, the passion and sense of rebirth he
> enjoyed with Tommaso soon subsided, and the artist's tormented
> struggle with death and the means of salvation continued to the end.
> (180)

These images, as interpreted by Liebert, do indeed make use both of
castration and reunion fantasies. Also consistent with the theme of
reunion with the father is an emphasis in his art on the negative
oedipal and homosexual elements, which lead us to make certain
inferences about Michelangelo's personality.

Spitz (1985), in critically discussing the view that a work of art is
mainly an expression of an iconographical tradition, noted that the
notion of the dynamic unconscious rebuts the anti-intentionalists' (or
culturalists') admonition to respect the integrity of a work of art
as only a consciously formed cultural object. Spitz's view correctly
recognizes the importance of the dynamically unconscious unresolved
conflicts as factors determining the final work of art. Steinberg, in
contrast, did not accord any particular power to unconscious factors,
such as castration anxieties, in constructing the iconology that has, as
its manifest content, the theme of the incarnation and such corollary
themes as the blood of the circumcision prefiguring the blood-hyphen
of the resurrection. A full psychoanalytic understanding of the iconography in Renaissance art would have castration anxiety and death
themes as a latent or dynamically unconscious content motivating
the creation and form of the images, along with the received theological and normatively based iconography of the times.

Steinberg (1983) was either not interested in unconscious motivations influencing artistic creation and interpretation, or believed them
to be of insignificant influence. Perhaps he was right in stating that
the iconographical content linking Christ's sexuality with the theo-

logical notions of incarnation and humanation of God was conscious and deliberate, only to be repressed in subsequent centuries because of political-religious upheavals in the Church. He did not give enough credit, though, to the potential for unconscious fantasies operating in artist and audience alike to seize on this particular consciously held and later repressed iconography as the same human potential that influenced the construction of that iconography in the first place. In the iconographical images of the Renaissance repertoire of theological conventions specific to resurrection themes, Christ was either seated near the cross with loincloth barely disguising his raised member, or stepping out of the tomb, erect, with flag and loincloth unfurled, and with his genitals a prominent focal point in the composition. Those compositions are the consciously formed cultural object of which Spitz speaks. According to Steinberg, the reference to genital flesh risen was itself *also* culturally conscious but later repressed by employing new compositional traditions or by overpaintings. One must also view the cultural continuity of unconscious meaning as of the wish for a perpetual erection or perpetual capacity for sensual pleasure after death, or for ecstatic reunion, or for resurrection of the lost object, as contributing to the *formation* and to the *repression* of the content of this consciously intended image. It is precisely because such fantasies influenced the formation of Renaissance images that they later, for reasons of universal personal conflict dovetailing with specific theological-historical conflict, had to be relegated to oblivion via massive cultural repression which also echoed the workings of the dynamic unconscious in the individuals sharing a common culture.

Liebert (1983) concluded that Michelangelo's work, particularly that related to themes of resurrection, as in his *Christ Risen,* was, in addition to homosexual conflicts, largely motivated by anxieties about his own mortality and his wish to be resurrected, personally, in the images that he created of Adam, Christ, and God. This particular interpretation of Michelangelo's fantasy, arrived at by application of the pathographic method to the artist's life and art works, is similar to my interpretation of the resurrection fantasies of my patient, Dr. D, by applying the method of psychoanalytic interpretation to his free associations and his fantasies as they emerged in the psychoanalytic situation. Like Michelangelo, Dr. D also was obsessively preoccupied with his eventually impending death, not from the age of forty, like Michelangelo, but from the age of seventeen. We also must not rule out the possibility, even the likelihood, that Michelangelo's preoccupations originated at an earlier age than that discovered by his biographers and pathographers.

In discussing the limits of pathography, Spitz said that "pathography ultimately fails to solve its own implicit problem. It never completely succeeds in showing us how it is that what is in the mind becomes the finished work of art—or how the transformation actually occurs" (1985, 50). She also noted that the problem is compounded when the artist is no longer alive and has not in fact been psychoanalyzed by the pathographer. If she is right, then the works of this would-be-artist patient, like the works of a bona-fide artist who is in analysis, would be an excellent case for the application of the pathographic method. It is not necessary to address how a fantasy goes through successive transformations to become a work of art when we are not dealing with the psychology of the creative process. In the case of Dr. D, we are dealing with what may be considered a craft, or at least a set of skills, and with a person who may be considered a craftsman or artisan. That is, his art is, technically speaking, not art, and the art that is truly art is something about which he only fantasized. A study of the would-be-artist surely circumvents the problem that occurs when the artist is very famous though no longer alive and has not in fact been analyzed by the pathographer. The interesting question now arises of how this work of mine might have been written if the illustrative case came from a real artist and not a surgeon aspiring to be one. What similar and what different countertransference potentials would there be? For one, the psychoanalyst's involvement in the reality of a genuine work of art, itself, its existence in a medium and a tradition, a reality external to the psyche of the artist, as opposed to the largely idiosyncratic context of Dr. D's work and hobbies, would inevitably produce a different countertransference potential. One also cannot rule out the presence of a shared fantasy between analyst and would-be-artist, or even certain bona-fide artists, for that matter: the fantasy of resurrection through a biographical narrative study that becomes part of the permanent psychoanalytic literature and guarantees the co-authors' "resurrection" through immortal preservation, analogous to the way a work of art is preserved in a museum.

Conclusion

$\mathcal{T}$his work on two broad categories of fantasies of love and death comes to a close with the renewed conviction that themes of love and death in life and art stimulate fantasies that reflect a wide variety of psychological processes that may be ordered on a continuum ranging from the normal to the pathological. The normative psychological variants of Liebestod fantasies and resurrection fantasies echo and are embedded in universal wishes as well as in accepted or received historical-cultural traditions. Those traditions, likewise, reflect the psychological normative of the individuals comprising, creating, and upholding the historical-cultural matrix which they at the same time reflect. The pathological variants express the idiosyncratic within the individual. Sometimes, of course, historical norms encourage individual pathology. More often, however, individual pathology represents a deviation from the historical cultural norm. Now, how do all of these abstractions translate into judgments about the normality or pathology of Liebestod and resurrection fantasies? Fantasies may be examined according to the level of ego functioning reflected in their enactments. The higher the level of ego functioning, the more normal, the lower the level, the more pathological. Each of the two classes of fantasy is, by and large, characterized by its own *specific* ego function.

In the case of Liebestod fantasies, explorations into the romantic agony of the love-death, most particularly in the Tristan legend, the "high tale of love and death," have indicated that the level of ego functioning accompanying the yearning for *merger* in the burning desire to die together with one who is passionately loved, determines the normality or pathology of the consequences of the fantasy. In Liebestod fantasies, varying levels of ego functioning may be detected in the characteristic wish to merge with the object of passionate love. It is the tension inherent in the conflict between the wish to merge and the fear of merging that lends the Liebestod fantasy its stamp of drama that has been incorporated into such love stories as the Celtic legend of Tristan and Iseult, the romantic songs and ballads of the medieval troubadours, and the great romantic operas. The accent, in the Liebestod, is on the conflicts around the wish to merge one's ego with an Other. Yearning to die together expresses the wish for a "good death" via reunion with a loved one by means of the revival of old symbiotic fusion states of oneness, bliss, and the paradise of tensionless existence together. In the case of resurrection fantasies, merging with an Other is not prominent. What is unique to them is the major wish to preserve and perpetuate the self, most often narcissistically, without particular regard to or for an Other. One may wish to be resurrected in order to rejoin a lost object or to resurrect a lost object, but in the wish for reunion, when expressed in resurrection fantasies, the accent is not so much on the wish to lose the ego in a fusion as it is on the wish to regain the lost object as a self-enhancing possession, warding off the "bad death" by extending one's worth and pleasures in a reunion in the afterlife.

In the case of Liebestod fantasies, what does one specifically look for in order to determine the level of ego functioning? The ego function is designated as pathological when the passionate yearning for merger affects the normally good level of relevant ego functions: perception of the other as existing in his or her own right—as possessing a separate identity—and judgment about the consequences of one's actions. For example, idealization of the Other, of Iseult, blurs Tristan's knowledge of her human frailties. The strength of his passion disorganizes his judgment about the consequences for his survival of his heroic feats in destroying obstacles to the love-merger. Sometimes, the love object in a Liebestod fantasy is a selfob-ject, adding the narcissistic dimension to the Liebestod fantasy. The various levels of ego functioning must be identified in order to locate the fantasy properly on a normal-pathological continuum. The wish for merger and fusion of one's own ego boundaries with those of an Other in painful states of longing and yearning blend from the nor-mal into the pathological. For example, in cases of unrequited love, a tendency to idealize and to lose one's self to the indifferent other would surely be pathological in those instances when it leads to a dissolution of the ego—not only of the sense of self as separate, but of all normal autonomous functioning. Often, these states of misery and unbearable longing in unrequited love, so poignantly sung by the medieval troubadours, are perpetuated by the blinded lover in a unbridled way. In these instances, the lover's ego manifests no inte-grated efforts to respond to the reality of the other's indifference. Pathology is demonstrated when the merger-seeking lover in the Liebestod is unable to function at normal levels of perception, judg-ment and reality-testing. Ego functioning is damaged and the being-in-love state rightly, in those circumstances, may be considered pathological.

Pathological being-in-love and normal being-in-love, then, can be distinguished in terms of the levels of ego functioning that accom-pany the passionate state. The pathological states are characterized by boundary fusions, pathological identifications and maladaptive or uncontrolled ego regressions. Perception is selectively blunted, judgment is impaired, and reality testing is marked by denial of flaws and by overvaluation of the beloved. The more normal condition of being-in-love is characterized by full separation-individuation, em-pathic identifications, boundary crossing, and flexibility in ego func-tioning despite longer or shorter moments of what, if characterologi-cal, would be considered pathological. In fact, the very behaviors, such as sadomasochistic attachments to the obstacles that foster love and usually might be considered pathological, may also be used in the service of adaptations. That is, the obstacles that could destroy love can, under optimal conditions, serve to preserve it. We saw examples of this adaptive variation of the beloved pain of the troubadours in the manifestly sadomasochistic phenomena and the comings and goings in passionate love that also serve to delineate self from Other via forays into merged states from which one emerges whole and better. Such an emergence out of merger is to be found in the typical boundary crossings in the passionate seeking of "love-death" states. Boundary crossings, as opposed to boundary fusions, refer to the normally empathic putting oneself in the place of the other in order to understand what the other is feeling and then to gratify. In love relations, a man must be able to imagine what a woman feels like and what she needs in order to gratify her sexually and emotionally. The woman must similarly be able to identify with the man. They do not "become" the other, however, as in pathological boundary fusion where distinctions are entirely lost and the resilience that permits crossing from being merged as one to emerging as separate individual beings is compromised. This distinction between crossing and fusion is crucial for understanding the outcomes of Liebestod fantasies—whether they eventuate in real or symbolic death, for example a murder-suicide pact, or whether they lead to creative mastery and object love. The comings and goings, the putting of obstacles in the way of fulfillment that in bad circumstances are sadomasochistic, in good circumstances of good ego functioning can serve to maintain the self-boundaries of individuation. There are oscillations rather than permanence in the controlled regressions required to shift from the pleasure of passionate merger back to the satisfactions of a delineated, individuated self. The Tristan legend and other courtly myths of romantic love are allegorical representations of more than just pathological subversion of the self to the excesses of erotic powers and passion. They are also at times the quintessential expression of the developmentally normal process of optimal psychological distance regulation. Derivatives of this process may be observed throughout the life-cycle in the relationships of lovers, particularly in their attempts to resolve the prototypical conflicts of the preoedipal period. These are repetitive attempts to find and refind that optimal balance between oneness and separateness, to master fears of engulfment, and to tame the needs for autonomous self-delineation.

Even in the psychologically and socially extreme situations of love-death suicide pacts, we need to ascertain the level of ego functioning before pronouncing the parties to the agreement as suffering from pathology. The double suicides of lovers that aim at reuniting in love after death offer no real possibilities of autonomous selfhood. Of course, suicide pacts between the partners in elderly and ailing couples are often a mark of practical realism and humane compassion between two people whose level of judgment and object relatedness is most high, even though they may be motivated by the same love-death wishes as couples who have suspended judgment about their well-being in a literal and pathological enactment of the Liebestod. The couple described by Ernest Jones who gave up attempts at self-survival and mutual rescue in Niagara Falls suffered from failed ego functioning in an apparent abulia, or loss of will. The masses who suspended ego functioning and died together, an extinguished population, in the Jonestown massacre and in the Davidian compound in Waco, Texas, were possessed by more questionable motivation than some terminally ill nonagenarian. There are devoted couples who lovingly assist each other in dying as they did in living, in order to avoid, say, the anticipated deterioration and humiliation of agonizing last days in a poorly run nursing home. This distinction does not reflect a social or moral judgment, but is intended to emphasize that certain specific social outcomes reflect varying levels of ego functioning of individuals, couples, and groups.

These concluding remarks intend to stress that the level and intensity of passion is not what distinguishes normal from pathological variants of Liebestod fantasy enactment. We have come a long way from regarding passionate love as an aberration of intensely driven madness, of sadomasochistic excesses, as simply a romantic agony of fatal perversions and deadly sex. In psychological fact, the work of the adaptively functioning ego is fueled by the same sexual and aggressive drives that characterize the more pathological, often sado-masochistic resolutions. These powerful and driving forces in passionate love relations do not necessarily exclude a loving concern for the object. In fact, there is nothing to indicate that intense impulses cannot be harnessed in the service of regard for self and others. It is only in the context of ego weakness that we can think of the heat of passion as extinguishing and annihilating the object. The less adaptively functioning ego is more likely to be overwhelmed by the force of the drives. The swain who is swept away by passions and unable to distinguish "I" and "Thou" loses his judgment under the sway of the drives. In both seeking of the "good" death, as via reunion, and warding of the "bad" death, a range of normal to pathological outcomes may be found.

Falling-in-love, or being-in-love, then, can be a *capacity* of the ego, and not, per se, a pathological aberration. In normal being-in-love, there is oscillation in the degree of passion in the forays between merger and individuation, between oneness and separateness in the self-experience and in representations of self and other. Normality, then, is characterized by the capacity for full separation-individuation, boundary-crossing, and flexibility in ego functioning. Liebestod fantasies, under such optimal psychological conditions, when realized in life, could lead to such positive outcomes as object love and the creative mastery of fatalism. In normal passionate states we are likely to find temporary suspension of certain ego functions, analogous to creative or "controlled" regressions. In such instances, being-in-love, in and of itself, even when it includes yearnings to die together in blissful merger with the beloved object, does not necessarily preclude a loving concern for the object over the long run. The death in those normal Liebestod yearnings is a "death," like "le petit mort," from which one will return to a better life. Extinguishing and annihilating life and self are not part of the fantasy or of its consequences when realized.

It is not quite accurate to attribute to the Liebestod the ego functioning related solely to merger with the object and to resurrection fantasies that ego functioning relevant solely to narcissistic self-preservative strivings. There is an important narcissistic dimension to Liebestod fantasies, as well, particularly when we are dealing with twin narcissism, and the search for a selfobject, perhaps a "doppelganger," in passionate quests. There are indeed states of being-in-love in which one loves the object as oneself, as discussed extensively in chapter 1 which dealt with the topic of narcissism, romanticism, and creativity, and in the extensive discussion of the twin narcissism of the Liebestod in chapter 2. New currents in psychoanalytic thinking, starting with Kohut's (1966, 1971) position that a line of narcissistic development parallels the object-libidinal line of development, view narcissism and object relatedness not as mutually exclusive but as separate axes of personality development. Most psychoanalysts have abandoned the old view that narcissism is merely a precursor of object relations and object love and, thereby, a developmental stage to be outgrown. Kohut, for one, regarded narcissistic libido as normally undergoing progressive transformations that are developmental accomplishments. This newer view can account for the simple observation that certain people who fall romantically in love — which may represent an expansion of the idealized or narcissistic self, as well as a wish for merger with an Other — are also capable of object love — of loving someone for whom he or she *is,* not simply as one *wished oneself to be,* ideally speaking. The state of being-in-love touches on narcissistic gratifications. Being enthralled with an Other in such a way that expands one's own sense of self is a prelude, often, to the more stable, settled-down state of enduring love. Mutually being "in thrall" may precede and persist contrapuntally with object love, sustaining it over time. In fact, the two modes of loving coexist precisely because they radiate from narcissistic and object-libidinal lines of development respectively. Thus, there can be narcissistic modes of relating in the Liebestod. Narcissistic issues around fantasies of love and death are not then the exclusive province of resurrection fantasies, but may be found to some extent in Liebestod fantasies as well.

The idea that narcissistic aspects of passion were not to be understood in a purely pejorative sense was also taken up by Andreas-Salomé (1922) in her discussion of the essential duality of narcissism. She stressed two important elements in narcissistic modes of loving. One, like a pathological Liebestod, has to do with self-love, which when excessive annihilates both self and object. The other, like a normal Liebestod, has to do with the "persistent feeling of identification with the totality" or fusion with an Other with shared values, ideals, and loves, which she says underlie "narcissistic transformation to artistic creativity" (5).

Being-in-love is a transitory state, and despite strong, normally narcissistic elements, is often experienced as a rational, durable, "mature genital object relationship" (Bak 1973). If Kohut was right in asserting that the establishment of a narcissistic self is a maturational achievement paralleling that of object love, then it is easy to see how states of loving and being-in-love both recapitulate earlier ego states and may coexist in the mature adult. It is the wish to recapture those early ego states that is the hallmark of the desire to die together with a loved one in the fantasies of love and death with predominant Liebestod themes.

~

In resurrection fantasies, studied in this work in an analysis of representations of resurrection themes in Renaissance art and in contemporary clinical psychoanalytic data, the relevant dimension of ego functioning relates more to narcissism, both normal and pathological, as traditionally understood. Steinberg's erection-resurrection equation, despite the phrase-coiner's insistence on its sole reference to Christ's incarnation, surely suggests this narcissistic dimension, in that the wish for eternal sexual pleasure serves narcissistic more than object-related ends. In the fantasy of being resurrected, or of extending one's life on earth perpetually and eternally via a return of life after death, the wish is most usually to assert or preserve the self. The primary concern is the wish for resurrecting one's self and one's work and other creations in an effort to achieve immortality. Even in the wish, so common in resurrection fantasies, to extend sexual pleasures and prowess in the afterlife, regard for the object, or even a focus on the object as important, as it is in Liebestod fantasies, definitely takes second place. Merger wishes that are so typical in the case of Liebestod fantasies are likely to be found only in the cases where there is a confluence of the two types of fantasies. An example would be the case in which the wish for reunion, and possibly for being sensually happy after death, underlies the urgency for preservation of the self in immortality, perpetuity, or resurrection. When a resurrection fantasy contains a wish for reunion with a loved one after death, if not for the actual act of *dying together,* that resurrection fantasy contains a Liebestod element. This notion of reunion via resurrection is usually found to include hopes of perpetual eroticism and ecstasy of love after death, as well as hopes for symbiotic merger and fusion. When there is a confluence of Liebestod and resurrection fantasies, as in Wagner's great Ring Cycle, the protagonists, in yearning for ecstatic sexual consummation through death, seek to fulfill themselves narcissistically and to gratify wishes for eternal merger and bliss. Liebestod fantasies of dying together may or may not include hopes of resurrecting the love relationship after death. In the confluence of the two types of love-death fantasies, the loss of ego functioning in the Liebestod merger may be seen as a means to resurrecting the relationship. In cases where we do not find a confluence of Liebestod and resurrection wishes, we are unlikely to find signs of wishes and fears of merger, for in those cases, we are dealing primarily with narcissistic wishes for the continuation of the self into perpetuity.

For those whose narcissism is particularly pronounced, manifest fears of annihilation of the self are prominent. When death anxieties touch on fears of self-annihilation, dreams of death center on ideas of resurrection of the self after death. For such individuals, the merger of the Liebestod is not a salient feature. Intensely passionate relations are sought not for the purpose of merger and temporary loss of self-other boundaries, but intense sexual passion is considered a means of *avoiding* the amniotic blur of losing one's own sense of identity through merger with a passionately loved other. Themes of death become associated with sexual passion as a reflection of anxieties about annihilation of one's sense of self as an individual existing *separately* from an enamored other. The wish to be roused from death is a version of the wish to be aroused, sexually. From the puns of Boccaccio on "la resurrezion de la carne" to Leo Steinberg's "erection-resurrection equation," dealing with narcissistic tensions preempts dealing with conflicts around merger and individuation. It is as though death and implied resurrection of the self are preferable to the love-death and the implied annihilation of the self through merger. Time and again, older men compulsively seek sexual encounters with younger women in the manifest hope of reviving their youthful potency and avoiding the (to them) narcissistically mortifying experience of aging and impotence. As was the case with Dr. D, the unconscious fantasy motivating such desperately seeking elders is to "die in the saddle" in the hopes of resurrecting the narcissistically gratifying potent self-image. "Le petit mort" becomes for them "un grand mort."

The ego functioning, then, that is most discernible amongst those, like Dr. D, whose lives are guided by powerfully motivating resurrection fantasies, relates to perpetuation of the self by using the passionately loved Other to ward off the "bad death," as opposed to the ego functioning amongst those with powerfully motivating Liebestod fantasies, which aims to seek the "good death" through merger with the object. In the case of Dr. D, we were indeed able to see how his pathological attempts at perpetuation of the self in his compulsive quest for sexual encounters was typified by grandiosity in narcissistically driven preoccupation with prolonging his life indefinitely and thereby defeating the reality of ordinary death. Broadly speaking, lovers yearn to die together for two related reasons: one is to express the wish for a "good" death via symbiotic union and merger and the other is to ward off and master the possibilities of a "bad" death and all that the latter may signify, symbolically. So, in both Liebestod and resurrection fantasies, passionate love, a merger with the object in the former, a flirting with "fatal attractions" and "femmes fatales" in the latter, serve narcissistic needs of avoiding an ordinary death.

Romantic love and existential anxieties have always been inextricably bound together. To love is to be aware of loss, and to be aware of loss inevitably brings the one who knows into an intimate connection with death. The high tale of love and death, with us from time immemorial, does have its various possibilities of resolution.

Notes

Notes to Chapter One

Chapter 1 is an expansion of my paper with the same title, published in the *Journal of the American Psychoanalytic Association* 23 (1975): 407–23. I thank the *Journal* for permission to publish parts of that article in this book.

1. For a comprehensive retelling of the legend, see Bedier (1945).

2. Dr. Martin Nass has helped me to formulate the crucial position of nonregressive elements in the creative process. He emphasized the nonregressive aspects of creativity in his work on music and psychoanalysis (1971), stating that the capacity for shifts in ego states and temporary dissolution of ego boundaries is most common among the creative, and that the structural point of view permits such cognitive shifts to be understood as part of normal functioning. The presence of early modes of ego organization does not necessitate the postulation of a regressive process. We could think analogously of regression to narcissistic states among those in love as essentially nonregressive, but as a part of the natural creative process of falling-in-love as preparatory to other phases. Whether or not this analogous process is more apt to occur in the particularly gifted is an issue that will undoubtedly be debated.

Notes to Chapter Two

This chapter expands on a paper printed in the *Journal of the American Psychoanalytic Association* 29 (1981): 607–30. I wish to thank the *Journal* for permission to reprint parts included in this chapter.

1. The version by Bedier (1945) is the comprehensive retelling of the legend incorporating the five separately authored versions by Robert of Rheims, Thomas de Bretagne, Eilhart von Oberg, Gottfried von Strassburg, and Beroul. I am indebted to Dr. Judith Isaac for providing me with a historical chart depicting sixteen different transformations of the legend occurring between the seventh-century Celtic fable and the 1945 Bedier version, including Wagner's 1857 opera, *Tristan und Isolde.*

Notes to Chapter Four

1. It is worth noting that Brünnhilde's mother, Erde, has also been in an endless sleep.

References

Alvarez, A. 1971. *The Savage God: A Study of Suicide*. New York and London: W. W. Norton, 1990.

Andreas-Salomé, L. 1922. The dual orientation of narcissism. *Psychoanalytic Quarterly* 31: 1–30.

Bach, S. 1985. *Narcissistic States and the Therapeutic Process*. New York and London: Jason Aronson.

———. 1994. *The Language of Perversion and the Language of Love*. Northvale, N.J. and London: Jason Aronson.

Bak, R. C. 1968. The phallic woman: The ubiquitous fantasy in perversions. *Psychoanalytic Study of the Child* 23: 15–36.

———. 1973. Being in love and object loss. *International Journal of Psychoanalysis* 54: 1–8.

Bedier, J. 1945. *The Romance of Tristan and Iseult*. New York: Pantheon.

Bellak, L., M. Hurvich, and H. K. Gediman. 1973. *Ego Functions in Schizophrenics, Neurotics, and Normals*. New York: Wiley.

Bergman, P., and S. Escalona. 1949. Unusual sensitivities in very young children. *Psychoanalytic Study of the Child* 3–4: 333–52. New York: International Universities Press.

Bergmann, M. S. 1971. Psychoanalytic observations on the capacity to love. In *Separation-Individuation: Essays in Honor of Margaret Mahler*, ed. J. B. McDevitt and C. F. Settlage, 15–40. New York: International Universities Press.

———. 1980. On the intrapsychic function of falling in love. *Psychoanalytic Quarterly* 49: 56–77.

———. 1987. *The Anatomy of Loving*. New York: Columbia University Press.

Binion, R. 1993. *Love beyond Death: The Anatomy of a Myth in the Arts*. New York and London: New York University Press.

Blacker, R. S. 1983. Death, resurrection, and rebirth: Observations on cardiac surgery. *Psychoanalytic Quarterly* 52: 56–72.

Blatt, S. J. 1978. Paradoxical representations and their implications for the treatment of psychosis and borderline states. Paper presented at meeting of the Institute for Psychoanalytic Training and Research, New York City, May 18, 1978.

Boccaccio, G. 1350a. *The Decameron*. Trans. J. Payne, New York: Random House, 1930.

Boccaccio, G. 1350b. *The Decameron*. Harmondsworth, Eng. and New York: Penguin Classics, 1972.

Bouvet, M. 1958. Technical variations and the concept of distance. *International Journal of Psychoanalysis* 39: 211–21.

Brodsky, B. 1957. Liebestod fantasies in a patient faced with a fatal illness. *International Journal of Psychoanalysis* 38: 13–16.

Cellini, B. 1558. *Autobiography*. Trans. George Bull. Harmondsworth, Eng. and New York: Penguin Books, 1956.

Cohen, J. M., trans. 1957. *The Life of Saint Teresa of Avila*. Harmondsworth, Eng. and New York: Penguin Books.

Dante Alighieri. 1294. *Vita Nuova*. Trans. M. Musa. Oxford and New York: Oxford University Press, 1992.

de Rougemont, D. 1956. *Love in the Western World*. New York: Pantheon.

———. 1963. *Love Declared: Essays on the Myths of Love*. New York: Pantheon.

Edelheit, H. 1974. Crucifixion fantasies and their relation to the primal scene. *International Journal of Psychoanalysis* 55: 193–99.

Engel, G. 1975. The death of a twin: Mourning and anniversary reactions. Fragments of ten years of self-analysis. *International Journal of Psychoanalysis* 56: 23–55.

Evans, W. N. 1953. Two kinds of romantic love. *Psychoanalytic Quarterly* 22: 75–85.

Flugel, J. C. 1953. Death instinct, homeostasis and allied concepts. *International Journal of Psychoanalysis* 34 (supp.): 43–74.

Freud, S. 1905. Three essays on the theory of sexuality. *Standard Edition* 7: 123–243. London: Hogarth Press, 1957.

———. 1908. Creative writers and daydreaming. *Standard Edition* 9: 141–53. London: Hogarth Press, 1959.

———. 1910. Leonardo da Vinci and a memory of his childhood. *Standard Edition* 11: 57–137. London: Hogarth Press, 1957.

———. 1911. Psychoanalytic notes on an autobiographical case of paranoia. *Standard Edition* 12: 2–82. London: Hogarth Press, 1958.

———. 1912. On the universal tendency to debasement in the sphere of love. *Standard Edition* 11: 177–90. London: Hogarth Press, 1957.

———. 1913. The theme of the three caskets. *Standard Edition* 12: 289–301. London: Hogarth Press, 1958.

———. 1914. On narcissism: An introduction. *Standard Edition* 14: 67–102. London: Hogarth Press, 1957.

———. 1915. Thoughts for the times on war and death. *Standard Edition* 14: 273–300. London: Hogarth Press, 1957.

———. 1916 [1915]. On transience. *Standard Edition* 14: 303–7. London: Hogarth Press, 1957.

———. 1917 [1915]. Mourning and melancholia. *Standard Edition* 14: 237–58. London: Hogarth Press, 1957.

———. 1919. The "uncanny." *Standard Edition* 17: 217–56. London: Hogarth Press, 1957.

———. 1923. The ego and the id. *Standard Edition* 19: 2–66. London: Hogarth Press, 1961.

———. 1926. Inhibitions, symptoms, and anxiety. *Standard Edition* 20: 75–174. London: Hogarth Press, 1959.

———. 1927. Fetishism. *Standard Edition* 21:148–57. London: Hogarth Press, 1961.

———. 1930. Civilisation and its discontents. *Standard Edition* 21: 57–105. London: Hogarth Press, 1961.

García Márquez, G., and L. Duque. *Miracle in Rome.* Screenplay shown on PBS, 1990.

Gediman, H. K. 1975. Reflections on narcissism, romanticism, and creativity. *Journal of the American Psychoanalytic Association* 23: 407–23.

———. 1981. On love, dying together, and Liebestod fantasies. *Journal of the American Psychoanalytic Association* 29: 607–30.

Goldin, F. 1964. *The Mirror of Narcissus in Courtly Love.* Ithaca: Cornell University Press.

Grabar, A. 1968. *Christian Iconography: A Study of Its Origins.* Princeton: Princeton University Press.

Greenacre, P. 1957. The childhood of the artist: Libidinal phase development and giftedness. In *Emotional Growth* 2: 479–504. New York: International Universities Press, 1971.

———. 1970. The transitional object and the fetish: With special reference to the role of illusion. In *Emotional Growth* 1: 335–52. New York: International Universities Press, 1971.

Hall, J. 1974. *Dictionary of Subjects and Symbols in Art.* New York: Harper and Row.

Henahan, D. 1990. A tribute to the late Leonard Bernstein: A prophet untimely honored. *New York Times,* October 21, Sec. B, p. 1, col.2.

Hermann, I. 1936. Clinging and going-in-search: A contrasting pair of instincts and their relation to sadism and masochism. *Psychoanalytic Quarterly* 4 (1976): 55–36.

Isakower, O. 1938. A contribution to the patho-psychology of phenomena associated with falling asleep. *International Journal of Psychoanalysis* 9: 331–45.

Jacobson, E. 1971. *Depression.* New York: International Universities Press.

John, N., ed. 1983. The Valkyrie by R. Wagner. Trans. A. Porter, 1976. Opera Guild Series No. 21. London and New York: John Calder/Riverrun.

———. 1984. Siegfried by R. Wagner. Trans. A. Porter, 1976. Opera Guild Series No. 28. London and New York: John Calder/Riverrun.

———. 1985. Twilight of the Gods by R. Wagner. Trans. A. Porter, 1976. Opera Guild Series No. 31. London and New York: John Calder/Riverrun.

Jones, E. 1911. On "dying together." With special reference to Heinrich von Kleist's suicide. In *Essays on Applied Psychoanalysis* 1: 99–105. London: Hogarth Press, 1951.

———. 1912. An unusual case of "dying together." In *Essays on Applied Psychoanalysis* 1: 106–11. London: Hogarth Press, 1951.

———. 1929. Fear, guilt, and hate. In *Papers on Psychoanalysis.* Boston: Beacon, 1961.

Joseph, E. D. 1959. An unusual fantasy in a twin with an inquiry into the nature of fantasy. *Psychoanalytic Quarterly* 28: 189–206.

Kaplan, L. J. 1978. *Oneness and Separateness.* New York: Simon and Schuster.

———. 1991. *Female Perversions.* New York: Doubleday.

Kernberg, O. F. 1977. Boundaries and structure in love relations. *Journal of the American Psychoanalytic Association* 25: 81–114.

Kligerman, C. 1972. Panel on "creativity." *International Journal of Psychoanalysis* 53: 21–30.

Kohut, H. 1966. Forms and transformations of narcissism. *Journal of the American Psychoanalytic Association* 14: 243–72.

———. 1971. *The Analysis of the Self*. New York: International Universities Press.

Krafft-Ebing, R. von. 1886. *Psychopathia sexualis*. Philadelphia: F. A. Davis.

Kris, E. 1952. *Psychoanalytic Explorations in Art*. New York: International Universities Press.

Kuhns, R. 1983. *Psychoanalytic Theory of Art: A Philosophy of Art on Developmental Principles*. New York: Columbia University Press.

Lawrence, D. H. 1928. *The Man Who Died*. In *The Later D. H. Lawrence* 399–449. New York: Alfred A. Knopf, 1952.

Lewin, B. D. 1946. Sleep, the mouth, and the dream screen. *Psychoanalytic Quarterly* 15: 419–34.

———. 1950. *The Psychoanalysis of Elation*. New York: Norton.

Liebert, R. S. 1983. *Michelangelo: A Psychoanalytic Study of His Life and Images*. New Haven: Yale University Press.

Lifton, R. J. 1979. *The Broken Connection*. New York: Simon and Schuster.

Mahler, M. S. 1972. Rapprochement subphase of the separation-individuation process. *Psychoanalytic Quarterly* 41: 487–506.

Mahler, M. S., F. Pine, and A. Bergman. 1975. *The Psychological Birth of the Human Infant*. New York: Basic Books.

Mailer, N. 1971. The prisoner of sex. *Harpers Magazine*, March, 41–92.

Millington, B. 1984. *Wagner*. Princeton, N.J.: Princeton University Press, 1992.

Morgenthau, H. J. 1962. Love and Power. In *The Restoration of American Politics*. Chicago: University of Chicago Press.

Nass, M. L. 1971. Some considerations of a psychoanalytic interpretation of music. *Psychoanalytic Quarterly* 40: 303–16.

Newman, E. 1924. *Wagner as Man and Artist*. New York: Alfred A. Knopf, Limelight, 1989.

Oremland, J. D. 1989. *Michelangelo's Sistine Ceiling: A Psychoanalytic Study of Creativity*. Madison, Conn.: International Universities Press.

Panofsky, E. 1939. *Studies in Iconology: Humanistic Themes in the Art of the Renaissance*. London: Oxford University Press. Icon Editions. Reprint, New York: Harper and Row, 1972.

Person, E. J. 1989. *Dreams of Love and Fateful Encounters*. New York: Penguin.

Plath, S. 1961. Daddy. In *Ariel: Poems by Sylvia Plath*. New York: Harper Perennial, 1965.

Polachek, C., ed. 1964. Salomé by R. Strauss. G. Schirmer's Collection of Opera Librettos. New York: G. Schirmer.

Pollock, G. H. 1975. On Mourning, immortality, and utopia. *Journal of the American Psychoanalytic Association* 23: 334–62.

——. 1976. Manifestations of abnormal mourning: Homicide and suicide following the death of another. *Annual of Psychoanalysis* 4: 225–49. New York: International Universities Press.

Praz, M. 1951. *The Romantic Agony*. London: Oxford University Press.

Puffet, D. 1984. "Siegfried" in the context of Wagner's opera writing. In *Siegfried, by R. Wagner*, ed. N. John. Opera Guild Series No. 28. London and New York: John Calder/Riverrun.

Schachtel, E. G. 1959. *Metamorphosis: On the Development of Affect, Perception, Attention, and Memory*. New York: Basic Books.

Schopenhauer, A. 1858. The metaphysics of sexual love. In *The World as Will and Representation*, trans. E. F. G. Payne. New York: Dover, 1966.

Schur, M. 1972. *Freud: Living and Dying*. New York: International Universities Press.

Shakespeare, W. 1623. *Twelfth night*. In *The Comedies, Histories, and Tragedies of Mr. William Shakespeare*, Illustrated Edition 1: 851–920. Chicago: Spencer Press, 1955.

Sill, G. G. 1975. *A Handbook of Symbols in Christian Art*. New York: Macmillan.

Skelton, G. 1983. A conflict of power and love. In *The Valkyrie, by R. Wagner*, ed. N. John. Opera Guild Series No. 21. London and New York: John Calder/Riverrun.

Smith, S. 1977. The golden fantasy: A regressive reaction to separation anxiety. *International Journal of Psychoanalysis* 58: 311–24.

Spitz, E. H. 1985. *Art and Psyche*. New Haven: Yale University Press.

Steinberg, L. 1983. *The Sexuality of Christ in Renaissance Art and in Modern Oblivion*. New York: Pantheon/October.

Tanner, M. 1985. An introduction to the end. In *Twilight of the Gods, by R. Wagner*, ed. N. John. Opera Guild Series No. 31. London and New York: John Calder/Riverrun.

Updike, J. 1963. More love in the western world. *New Yorker*, August 24: 90–104.

——. 1994. *Brazil*. New York: Alfred A. Knopf.

von Westernhagen, C. 1978. *Wagner: A Biography*. Cambridge: Cambridge University Press, 1981.

Warner, M. 1976. *Alone of All Her Sex: The Myth and the Cult of the Virgin Mary*. New York: Vintage Books, 1983.

White, K. S. 1981. *Onward and Upward in the Garden.* New York: Farrar Straus Giroux.

Wilder, T. 1927. *The Bridge of San Luis Rey.* New York: Avon, 1976.

———. 1938. *Our Town.* New York: Harper Perennial, 1985.

Winnicott, D. W. 1953. Transitional objects and transitional phenomena. In *Collected Papers: Through Paediatrics through Psychoanalysis,* 229–42. New York: Basic Books, 1958.

———. 1958. The capacity to be alone. In *The Maturational Processes and the Facilitating Environment,* 29–36. New York: International Universities Press, 1965.

Zilboorg, G. 1938. The sense of immortality. *Psychoanalytic Quarterly* 7: 171–79.

Author Index

Subject Index